Kapila's Sāmkhya

Patañjali's Yoga

Theory and Practice
Third Edition

Inspired from Lectures of
Brahmrishi Vishvatma Bawra

Compiled and Edited by
William and Margot Milcetich

Brahmrishi Yoga Publications

Originally published as Kapil's Sāmkhya Patañjali's Yoga, Brahmrishi Yoga
Publications, 2008
Revised 2012.
Third Edition 2018

Publisher: Brahmrishi Yoga Publications
c/o BrahmrishiYoga.org

For information, contact brahmrishiyoga.org

Library of Congress Control Number: 2012906241
ISBN: 978-1475127850

Acknowledgement

We stand in awe of this ancient, oral tradition and we are indebted to our Guru's insights that made this knowledge accessible to us.

We are greatly indebted to the literary skills of many people over the years, most recently Lisa Thiel and Keith Lazuka in this third edition. Their dedication and sincere efforts to grasp and preserve the meaning have enriched this presentation.

In honor of Swami Bawra's vision for education, all proceeds of this book will go to a free school established by him in Jabalpur, India. Didi Gyaneshwari has brought the vision of Swami Bawra into a flourishing reality. Brahmrishi Yoga is delighted to participate in this unfoldment.

William & Margot Milcetich

Contents

Preface i

Introduction 1

Sāmkhya

    How to Remove Pain 6

    1. Eight Root Causes 7

    2. Sixteen Modifications 10

    3. Purusha 11

    4. Three Attributes 14

    5. Evolution and Involution 17

    6. Three Causes of Suffering 19

    7. Five Sources of Knowledge 21

    8. Five Causes of Action 22

    9. Five Winds 24

    10. Five Essences of Action 25

    11. Five Knots of Ignorance 27

    12. Twenty-eightfold Inabilities 29

    13. Nine Satisfactions 30

    14. Eight Gifts 31

    15. Ten Root Objects 33

    16. Emanation is Accumulation 38

    17. Fourteen States of Manifested Beings 42

    18. Threefold Bondage 45

    19. Threefold Liberation 48

    20. Three Proofs 49

    21. Conclusion 50

Yoga

Samadhi Pada/Stable Intellect

    I/1-I/4 Definition of Yoga 53

    I/12-I/22 Practice and Detachment 66

    I/23–I/51 Devotional Practice 82

Sadhana Pada/Practice

    II/1-II/27 Integrated Practice 108

    II/28-II/55 Eight Limbed Path 139

Vibhuti Padi/Accomplishments

    III/1-III/3 Dhāranā, Dhyāna, Samādhi 167

Glossary 175

Bibliography 182

Preface

Brahmrishi Vishvatma Bawra was born in a small Indian village near Varanasi in 1934. As a child, he shied away from school and had no formal education. At the age of eighteen, he was enlightened by the touch of a great *yogi*, Bhagvan Chandra Mauli, and remembered many previous lives spent with his guru. Under his guru's guidance, Swami Bawra left his family to study higher spiritual practices in Ayodhya at the principal center of the Vaishnava Order. By the grace of his master he received a distinctive memory of scripture and philosophical treatises. He became a learned *yogi* of the Vaishnava Sanyasi Order. After a period of time, his master insisted he return to society and help humanity.

Swami Bawra hesitated to leave his spiritual ecstasy, but followed his master's guidance. With only a loincloth and a small bag with Holy Scriptures, he traveled throughout India begging alms and giving lectures on the *Bhagavad Gītā*, *Rāmāyana*, Upanishads, Sāmkhya, Yoga, and Vedānta philosophies. In his lectures, he shared philosophy in the light of modern science. After twelve years of wandering, at the request of his disciples, Swami Bawra agreed to establish a center for spiritual practice. The first center was inaugurated in 1965, and his mission eventually became an international organization. Swami Bawra also founded numerous schools to provide education for poor children in the villages of India.

Swami Bawra's teachings emphasize the spiritual science of *Brahma Vidyā*, knowledge of the source of life in *Brahman*, which has two aspects, theory and practice. In the Upanishads and *Bhagavad Gītā*, the theory is called Sāmkhya, and its practical aspect is called Yoga. On the basis of his own experiences, Swami Bawra taught *Maha Yoga*, an integrated practice of thought and breath for realizing self and finding freedom from suffering.

Swami Bawra traveled to the United States, Canada, and England to share his knowledge. Margot and I studied with him when he traveled, and we periodically went to India to study and meditate with him there. Swami Bawra encouraged me to remain in my professional career while continuing a practice of deep meditation and regular study. Margot began teaching meditation in 1976 and became a yoga teacher in 1982. For many years, we have jointly led meditation and study sessions based on Swami Bawra's teachings.

In 2005, Margot founded Brahmrishi Yoga Teacher Training. Swami Bawra's inspiration and guidance on the need for Western practitioners to understand Sāmkhya is the core of this training. In 2006, I retired from my

i

professional career and began to teach meditation and assist with philosophical presentations. We both felt a need for an English commentary incorporating Swami Bawra's revival of Sāmkhya as the basis for our teaching.

Margot had compiled and edited a series of lectures given on *Tattva Samasa*, a brief outline of Kapila's Sāmkhya. She wanted this worked into a presentation on the practices enumerated in the *Yoga Sūtras* to highlight and emphasize their philosophical basis. Subsequently, I found additional lectures Swami Bawra had given on *Tattva Samasa*. This commentary on Sāmkhya is a compilation of all these lectures, as well as additional supplemental material.

Likewise, the Yoga section is compiled from lectures on the first two chapters of *Patañjali's Yoga Sūtras*. I collected, transcribed, compiled, and edited this material, supplementing it with previous works and other lectures of Swami Bawra to create this commentary.

Our intent is to provide an understanding of the philosophical foundation and practical methods for achieving inner freedom. We begin with a commentary on *Tattva Samāsa*, which outlines Kapila's philosophy and serves as the theoretical base necessary for understanding Yoga. This is followed by a selection of Patañjali's *Yoga Sūtras*, which illuminate the aim, principles and methods of Yoga.

William Milcetich

Pronunciation: To assist English readers with the pronunciation of frequently used Sanskrit terms, letters have been added to the strict transliteration of Sanskrit to English. For example, *puruśa* is written as *purusha* and *prakriti* as *prakriti*. The long vowels of a, i, and u are indicated by the symbols, ā, ī, and ū and the sh sound is indicated by ś.

Introduction

There are six systems of Vedic thought that pair to form three primary philosophical schools. Each of these systems relies on and interprets the Vedas,[1] ancient texts of knowledge realized by the seers thousands of years ago. All systems summarize the gist of their teaching in the form of short *sūtras*, which theorize the cause of life and offer a practical means for living free from suffering. Commentaries explain and elaborate on the meaning of these *sūtras*.

The oldest school is Sāmkhya, an analysis of nature and spirit, paired with Yoga, a treatise on method. Vaiśesika, atomic theory, is linked to Nyāya, logic. Vedānta, a theory of absolute truth, pairs with Pūrva Mīmāmsā, duty. The original teachers of these systems are Kapila of Sāmkhya and Hiranyagarbha of Yoga; Kanada of Vaiśesika and Gautama of Nyāya; and Vyāsa of Vedānta and Jaimini of Pūrva Mīmāmsā. There are no written documents credited to Hiranyagarbha, so we are indebted to the work of Patañjali who compiled the ancient teaching of Yoga.

Paired Schools of Vedic Thought

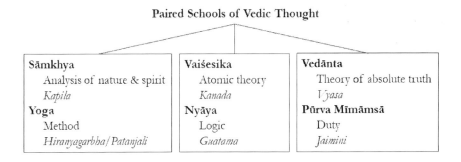

Sāmkhya	**Vaiśesika**	**Vedānta**
Analysis of nature & spirit	Atomic theory	Theory of absolute truth
Kapila	*Kanada*	*Vyasa*
Yoga	**Nyāya**	**Pūrva Mīmāmsā**
Method	Logic	Duty
Hiranyagarbha / Patanjali	*Guatama*	*Jaimini*

Sāmkhya and Yoga teach that the cause of this universe is both nature and spirit. When a person achieves pure wisdom and discerns the distinct and eternal coexistence of nature and spirit, he or she will realize ultimate truth, be free from suffering, and gain emancipation. Nyāya and Vaiśesika accept the gross elements as causal reality, and emphasize logic as the means for realizing truth. When a seeker becomes fully aware of both God and the visible world, he or she is freed from suffering. This is the path of God realization, but it relies on logic, not belief. Vedānta and Pūrva Mīmāmsā teach that the cause of this universe is *Brahman*, which manifests

---

[1] *Veda* means knowledge.

by means of its divine power, *maya*. When a seeker realizes supreme *Brahman* as ultimate truth and performs appropriate actions, the seeker realizes that the soul is not separate from *Brahman*, and achieves freedom from suffering.

There is controversy regarding the development of Sāmkhya philosophy. The accepted oral tradition of Sāmkhya is that Kapila was the original teacher and expounder of this philosophy. After teaching this knowledge to his mother, Devhuti, he taught Āsuri, who taught Pañcaśikha. Pañcaśikha was the first to compile the Sāmkhya philosophy in a manuscript called the *Sastritantra*. The *Sastritantra* was lost during the passage of time. A collection of twenty-two aphorisms attributed to Pañcaśikha were collected and compiled from various sources. This is called *Pañcaśikha-Sūtram*. These twenty-two aphorisms are considered related with what Kapila taught.

The most well-known text on Sāmkhya is the *Sāmkhya Kārikā* of Īśvarakrsna[2] completed during the 2nd century C.E. Additionally, there is the *Sāmkhya-Pravachana Sutram* containing 572 verses and a brief outline called *Tattva Samāsa*, which is used in this work to explain the philosophy of Sāmkhya.

Accepting nature as real characterizes Sāmkhya. Sāmkhya is an analysis of two parallel forces, *prakriti* and *purusha*, nature and spirit. Sāmkhya philosophy accepts the reality of the force, movement, and laws of nature, as distinct from, but not lesser than spirit. According to Sāmkhya, nature provides the means for *purusha*, the indwelling spirit, to gain experience and emancipation. *Purusha* remains as one infinite consciousness, even when expressing through the media of nature.

The concept of nature, or *prakriti*, is contained in the term *avyakta*, as found in the *Katha Upanishad*. *Avyakta* means invisible or unmanifest cause. Nature is the causal phenomenon of the manifested world. It is that by which the world is projected, and it is that into which this projection disappears. Nature is the source of all that receives the light of *purusha*.[3] According to Sāmkhya, manifestation occurs first in the causal matter of *mahatattva* and *buddhi*, the cosmic intellect and the individual intellect. Yoga uses the term *chitta* for these media of manifestation. These terms indicate

---

[2] Brahmrishi Vishvatma Bawra's commentary on the *Sāmkhya Kārikā* is available in print.
[3] *Katha Upanishad* I.3.10-11.

the first evolution of nature, which is the medium for the manifestation of consciousness.

The medium, whether it is called *buddhi* or *chitta*, adopts the qualities of all-pervasive consciousness, which are truth, knowledge, and infinity.[4] Other terms for these qualities are existence, intelligence, and bliss. In the Vedas, an example of an iron ball is given to describe how nature captures consciousness.[5] Because an iron ball has the potential to receive the element of fire, it looks like a ball of fire when it is placed in flames. In the same way, the medium of nature has the potential to adopt the qualities of consciousness. As the iron ball can receive and adopt fire, likewise the medium has the natural ability to receive consciousness from *purusha* and adopt its qualities. *Purusha*, spirit, is one and absolute. The media are countless. When the medium receives and adopts consciousness as its own, that enlivened medium is called *jīvātmā*, individual being, or soul.

Sāmkhya does not believe that the world was created by a specific power; it is a projection of nature inspired by spirit, as natural as ripples appearing in water. This natural process is eternal. When manifestation occurs, both nature and spirit appear in causal form, which is called cosmic intellect or cosmic *chitta*. In other traditions, this is called God. In Yoga this manifestation is called *Īśvara*. This level is called the supreme cause because it is from here that the universe projects into form. The individual soul is like a ray of light from this supreme cause. This understanding is the foundation of the path of devotion, which is one of the methods taught in the *Yoga Sutras*.

At the heart of Sāmkhya lies the theory of causation: the effect must reside within the cause. If an effect does not reside in the cause, then it can never be expressed by that cause. The potential for a clay pot resides in clay. Clay is essential for the formation of a clay pot, and the pot is a transformation or an effect of the causal substance of clay. The source of all forms lies in *prakriti*, and the source of consciousness lies in *purusha*.

Sāmkhya means "to know distinctly." The essence of Sāmkhya philosophy is that all manifestations of life can be traced back to their origin in nature and spirit. The goal of this philosophy is to see clearly with wisdom in order to end suffering. The projection of nature is examined

---

[4] The Upanishads describe *purusha* as *satyam jñānam anantam*: truth, knowledge, and infinity. *Taittirīya Upanishad* II.1.2.
[5] *Rig* and *Yajur Vedas*.

thoroughly. The manifestation of spirit is realized. Knowledge of the parts is emphasized to understand the whole. Sāmkhya's emphasis on the particulars of nature and its differentiation from spirit provides the basis for our understanding of our human experience. With this understanding, we can curtail our misidentification of consciousness with the medium of nature.

Through the process of enumerating the parts, Kapila establishes the self as the knower, which is one with consciousness. The observation of the force, movement, and laws of nature becomes a practice of withdrawing our identification with each part. When we identify with partial experience, we feel insecure due to the intrinsic changeable quality of nature. When we realize consciousness as separate from the qualities of nature, we realize our inherent wholeness. We become stable in an experience of infinite consciousness, rather than caught in an impermanent identification with the enumerated objects. By realizing the difference between nature and spirit, and by understanding the nature of the true self, we can live in the light of our own wisdom and be free from suffering. It is my belief that in the light of Sāmkhya, humankind can achieve happiness in the world and reach salvation.

Yoga accepts the principles of Sāmkhya and uses its categories and classifications, but there are some generally accepted differences between Yoga and Sāmkhya. Sāmkhya sees the world as a projection of nature inspired by spirit. Yoga is theistic in its inclusion of *Īśvara* or the supreme cause. Sāmkhya is considered theoretical while Yoga gives practical methods. Both Yoga and Sāmkhya encourage us to seek the truth through our own experience. There is a danger in belief without experience.

The chief aim of human life is to eliminate suffering and find happiness. Because of ignorance and illusion, we turn outward through the senses toward the world of objects as a way of fulfilling the inner demand for wholeness. The sages of India provide the example of a musk deer to explain this behavior. The aroma of musk is so alluring that when a stag's sensitive nose catches it, he roams the forest day and night seeking its source. He exhausts himself in a fruitless quest chasing the sweet fragrance never realizing the source is within him.

Likewise, we engage in various activities trying to fulfill our desire for eternal happiness, but instead we experience constant restlessness. This restlessness in the mind will never be removed until the desire for lasting happiness is fulfilled, and that is only possible when we realize oneness with the supreme cause. Just as eating food simultaneously brings satisfaction, nourishment, and the absence of hunger, the experience of the real self brings satisfaction, knowledge, and freedom from the feeling of separation. In order to have this realization, we have to train the body, mind, and breath.

Sāmkhya and Yoga help us understand our current situation and reveal an ideal that is within our reach. We must become aware of truth and then set out toward our ideal. We are human beings with the ability to discriminate. We have an intellect, ego, mind, senses, and a body that can be used for our upliftment.

Practice is the effort to search for the real self and inherently requires detachment. Detachment does not mean abandoning one's duties and responsibilities. It is a process of releasing the self from dependency on external stimulation. In this way we are able to be more impartial and therefore skillful in action. Sāmkhya philosophy provides the underlying framework for understanding the self as the seer, distinct from the seen. It describes life as a projection of nature and spirit, and explains that we need to understand both of these in order to be established in the self.

The heart of a practice is *sraddhā*, a deep and steadfast faith. Every action is driven by intention. Our success in Yoga comes with the belief that the continuity of our efforts will bring happiness. The goal is to eliminate the feeling of lack or separateness that arises from our identification of our true self, the seer, with the material world, the seen. When we realize the seer is one with consciousness and is an observer of all activity, we are freed from the feeling of separation.

My intent in this commentary is to provide an understanding of the philosophical framework and practical methods for achieving inner freedom. I begin with a commentary on Kapila's *Tattva Samāsa*,[6] twenty-two *sūtras*, attributed to Lord Kapila, which form the theoretical foundation for understanding practice. This is followed by a selection of Patañjali's *Yoga Sūtras*.

---

[6] The *sūtras* of *Tattva Samāsa* are presented as listed in *The Samkhya Philosophy* translated by Nandalal Sinha, Oriental Books Reprint Corporation, 1915.

Tattva Samāsa

1

athātah tattva samāsah
Now, how to remove pain—the Nutshell Principles

Atha is an auspicious word in Sanskrit, and many philosophical treatises begin with it. It is translated as "now." The word establishes the authority of the speaker and a mastery of the subject, and it calls us to be present.

Atah indicates the essence of this teaching: it is a method to remove pain. Everyone desires to annihilate pain and live in pleasure. Our inner demand is for painless pleasure, but we experience both pain and pleasure. When we are in pain, we are not free to enjoy pleasure. Even the fear of pain inhibits our pleasure. As a result, we mostly live in fear of pain and hoping for pleasure. We hope one day pain will disappear and leave only pleasure in its place. Kapila offers us a method for removing pain and living in happiness independent of the cycle of pleasure and pain.

Suffering is not part of our essential nature and, therefore, it can be removed from our lives. If pain were the nature of the self then it could not be removed. Just as heat is an essential property of fire and cannot be separated from fire, our natural properties can never be separated from us.

Conversely, whatever is not a natural part of the self is alien and can be removed. Like a metallurgic process where heat is applied to remove impurities, our lives can be purified because whatever is not intrinsic can be removed. Pain attaches to the self, but because it is alien, it can be weeded out. The great evidence that pain is alien is that we want to be rid of it. When we feel pain we want relief. Pain motivates us to search for its cause and discover how it comes into our lives. This treatise on Sāmkhya helps us in our search.

Tattva Samāsa means the gist of truth, or succinct principles of truth. Kapila teaches Sāmkhya in a concise form. These nutshell principles reveal our true nature and the impurities that cause our suffering. These teachings show us how to discriminate the cause of our misery. There are two ways to encompass these teachings, *vyāsa* and *samāsa*. *Vyāsa* means, "in broad form and in much detail," and *samāsa* means "in a nutshell form." These teachings illuminate the search for truth in a nutshell form, *tattva samāsa*.

Only a determined and discerning person will be able to crack into these small, subtle nutshells of wisdom. Philosophical treatises demand clear thought. Many of us have presumptions, and we do not want to let them go, even though they have brought us pain. My teacher instructed me to keep my mind free when studying philosophy. We should not cling to our old ideas. Instead of correlating and comparing our assumptions as we hear the new ideas, we must open our minds and listen. After we take the teaching in, we must see how it can nourish us. Just as a cow eats and then quietly chews, gradually assimilating the food, we must take in these teachings piece by piece, gradually digesting what we have learned. After listening, after understanding, continue to think upon it.

Without absorbing and reflecting on a subject, listening is useless. And without meditating on the subject once it is understood, thinking is also useless. Listen, receive the knowledge, examine it again and again, and meditate on your understanding. Then the knowledge will be yours. If we only listen and repeat what we have heard without our own realization, then we gain no wisdom.

The *Sāmkhya Kārikā* of Īśvarakrsna indicates the essential method for gaining freedom from suffering is to develop refined discrimination between three things: the manifest, the unmanifest and knower.[7] The manifest, *vyakta*, is everything that is visible and perceptible. The unmanifest, *avyakta,* is the source of whatever is visible and perceptible. This is also called *prakriti* or causal nature. The knower of both the manifest and unmanifest is called *jña* in the *Sāmkhya Kārikā*. In this treatise, the term for the knower is *purushah*, spirit.

~~~

2
kathayāmi ashtau prakritayah
There are eight root causes:
nature, intellect, ego, sound, touch, form, taste and smell

In Sāmkhya philosophy there are two eternal truths, called *purusha* and *prakriti*, spirit and nature. This *sūtra* introduces nature, *prakriti*. Kapila describes nature first because it is visible and easier to analyze, whereas spirit is invisible and difficult to comprehend. Our embodied soul becomes attached to the physical world and it is challenging for us to

---

[7] *Sāmkhya Kārikā* II.

suspend our interest in the physical world in order to reach toward the metaphysical world. According to Sāmkhya, when we are fully aware of nature, we can know and realize spirit.

Prakriti or nature is the causal phenomenon of the manifested world. *Prakriti* has three attributes: light, movement and stability. The roots *pra, kr,* and *iti,* are found in the terms for the *gunas. Sattoguna* is *prakash,* luminous light. *Rajoguna* is *kriya,* subtle movement. *Tamoguna* is *sthiti,* stability. The three *gunas* are *pra-kr-iti,* nature. *Prakriti's* attributes cause nature to transform into effects and create forms. This universe is a projection of nature. Causal nature is unmanifest, beyond vision, beyond perception, beyond everything. One can only infer the existence of causal nature by its projection into form.

Scientists declare that energy is the cause of the material word. Although scientists cannot explain what energy is, they are able to define it by what it is not. They describe energy as formless, weightless, colorless, and limitless. No scientist can show you energy. We can only know it, study it, by its effects. Unmanifest energy is beyond our vision and perception, and the first manifestation of energy is also beyond our vision and perception. With the naked eye we cannot see atoms, nor can we see the electrons, protons, and neutrons of which atoms are made. With the naked eye we only see combinations of atoms.

Although the projection of nature gives the appearance of diversity, nature is fundamentally one infinite power. As nature manifests in the world, it projects through eight root causes. A root cause is something that projects into something new. Among the eight, *prakriti* alone is pure, meaning that it is not the effect of something but is purely causal. Nature is the causal phenomena of this universe. The other seven root causes are mixed, as they are both an effect of one thing and the cause of something else.

The first of these seven mixed causes is *mahat. Mahat* is a medium. It holds impressions of experience, which forms *buddhi.* Both terms are translated as intellect. Intellect is an English approximation for *buddhi. Buddhi* names both the location of the intellect as well as its functions, which are thinking and deciding. Intellect is the first manifestation of nature. The impressions held by the intellect structure our beliefs and form our ability to discriminate and make judgments. It is the effect of unmanifest nature and it is the cause of ego, *ahamkāra.*

8

Ahamkāra is the projection of these impressions into patterns of behavior and tendencies toward what we like and away from what we dislike. *Ahamkāra* includes our skills and abilities to achieve what we want and protect ourselves from our aversions. It is the form of our innate nature and inherent disposition. The active attribute of nature, *rajoguna*, is predominant in *ahamkāra* as the performer or agent of action. Ego is the effect of intellect and the cause of the subtle elements. Sound is the effect of ego and it is the cause of touch. Touch projects into form, form gives rise to taste and taste projects into smell.

These last five root causes are called subtle matter, *tanmātra*. *Tanu* means subtle, and *mātra* means matter. The *tanmātras* are the intermediary stages of causal energy's transformation into the physical universe. These subtle elements are the effects of ego and each one is the cause of one of the primordial elements: space, air, fire, water and earth respectively. Sound is first and causes space, touch causes air, form causes fire, taste causes water, and smell causes earth. Subtle matter is the cause of gross matter. Everything we see in gross form is a bundle of subtle energy.

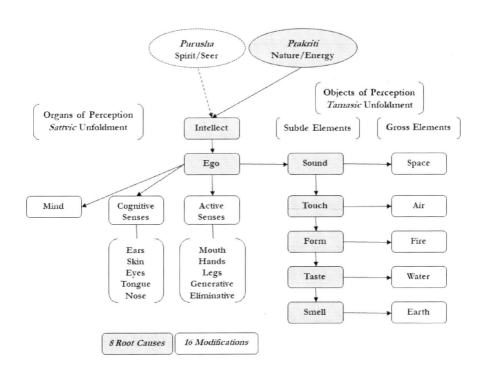

9

Nature is the causal phenomenon of the universe. Everything in existence can be traced back to one unmanifest power: nature. The first seven evolutions of unmanifest nature cause other projections and are part of the transformation of causal nature. Together these eight root causes transform into all other modifications of nature.

~~~

3
sodaśakah tu vikārah
Sixteen modifications: mind, five cognitive senses,
five active senses and five primordial elements

The eight root causes together are the subtle cause of the evolution of energy into sixteen modifications and, by extension, all of gross matter. *Vikārah* is a special word in this philosophy, meaning the transformation or modification of cause into effect. The metaphor given to illustrate this principle is the process of turning milk into yogurt. Milk is the cause and yogurt is the *vikārah*, a transformation, of milk. In the same way, the eight root causes transform into sixteen modifications. These sixteen modifications are the effects, and they do not produce anything new.

The predominant power of ego, which is *rajoguna*, unfolds in one of two ways, depending on whether there is the influence of *sattva* or *tamas*. The mind,[8] five cognitive senses and five active senses are extensions of the ego and considered to be the *sattvic* unfoldment.

The *tamasic* unfoldment of the ego causes sound. Sound becomes the cause of touch, touch causes form, form causes taste, and taste causes smell. These five *tanmātras* are vibrations that produce the five primordial elements. Waves of sound produce space. Sound creates space, and space creates nothing. Touch creates air and air creates nothing. Form creates fire and fire creates nothing. Taste creates water and water creates nothing. Smell creates earth and earth creates nothing. These elements are modifications and in different combinations they manifest in diverse ways, but in and of themselves they do not evolve to create anything new.

We can begin to understand this process by considering taste and water. When we think about something sweet, our salivary glands produce

---

[8] Mind is called the sixth cognitive sense or highest perceptive sense. Mind is a projection of ego. Ego without projection is pure I-amness or a sense of individual existence. Ego manifests in waves of thought (*vrittis*) called mind.

saliva even though no physical substance is present. Liquid is caused by thinking of the subtle vibration of taste.

The eight root causes and sixteen modifications constitute twenty-four aspects of nature. Causal nature is the unmanifest and these twenty-three effects are the manifest, from subtle to gross. The effects constitute the visible and perceptible world. All of these can be known. This philosophy is named Sāmkhya because it enumerates these projections. Sāmkhya means to know distinctly. The philosophy identifies the projections of nature, and from this we can analyze all of nature.

Through the effects we can search for the cause. In meditation we observe our relationship with the senses and slowly we begin to understand the mind. By observing the mind, we find the ego. We can approach the ego through any sense, because ego is the cause. All eleven senses and the five *tanmātras* are the effects of the ego. Each gross element projects from one *tanmātra*, and these originate from the ego. These sixteen effects are the means for approaching the cause. By analyzing one sense we can enter into its cause, gradually reaching up to ego, enabling us to understand who is using the sense.

Sāmkhya accepts that we live in the physical world and with discernment we can understand these activities of nature and reach a point where we recognize a distinct and separate knower.

~ ~ ~

4
purushah
Spirit

Sāmkhya is based on the theory of causation. Two principles of this theory are: (1) when there is correct analysis of an effect, the effect will lead us to its cause; and (2) the effect retains the qualities and properties of its cause. Kapila introduces nature first because it is visible and easier to understand. He teaches that there are eight root causes that produce sixteen effects, and the effects are the means for approaching the cause.

The analysis of an effect leads us to ego. The five *tanmātras* with the correlated primordial elements, the mind, the five perceptive and the five active senses all originate from ego. Through analysis we can observe who is interacting with these effects. When approaching ego and the discerning intellect, we are aware of consciousness. Consciousness has the capacity to be sentient and animated. The question arises: is consciousness a property of nature?

Because the intellect adopts the properties of consciousness it appears as if it is conscious. Likewise, the internal functions of ego and mind appear conscious. Analysis is a function of the intellect; the ego accepts or rejects; and the mind speculates or imagines. When, in the absence of sound, we think of sound, our abstract thoughts or emotions are separate from actual sound. Our thoughts and sentiments about sound, touch, form, taste, or smell and their related objects are not the property of the five elements, but the function of the mind, ego and intellect.

The intellect analyzes and examines emotions and feelings, which are displayed in the mind. Ego is active, accepting or rejecting the stimulation. We can observe and analyze our reactions. When we ask ourselves "Who am I?" our intellect determines the answer, not the ego or the mind. Our mind displays all information from the senses and our evaluation of experience. Sāmkhya teaches that the mind, ego, and intellect are separate and have their own distinct functions.

When nature appears in the forms of space, air, fire, water, and earth, it loses its capacity to be conscious. According to the theory of causation, if consciousness were a quality of nature it would not be lost at any stage. The cause always exists in the effect. The cause can exist without the effect, but the effect cannot exist without its cause. Without waves the calm ocean is present, but without the ocean there are no waves. If nature loses consciousness at any level of manifestation, then consciousness is not a property of nature. Consciousness must be separate from nature.

Then what is the source of consciousness? Kapila answers *purushah*. According to Sāmkhya there are two root causes of this universe: nature and spirit. Both are eternal and live side-by-side Nature is considered inanimate and insentient, while spirit or *purusha* is animate and sentient. Because nature is insentient and without consciousness, there must be another entity that is conscious and able to observe and know. This sentient awareness, *purusha*, is separate from insentient nature, and these two must be known distinctly.

Sāmkhya philosophers declare that without supreme spirit, life has no existence. The objects of the senses, the senses, mind, ego, and intellect are all enlightened by supreme consciousness. Krishna describes this property of *purusha* in the *Bhagavad Gītā* as: "Light of all lights, beyond darkness, the

12

knowable, and the goal of all knowledge, seated in the hearts of all."[9] So this one word, *purusha*, indicates the enlightener.

In the Vedas, we find descriptions of *purusha*. They include: (1) The one who is resting in this body is called *purusha*; (2) *Purusha* is consciousness; (3) The active consciousness that is making the body perfect is called *purusha*; and (4) The true form of *purusha* is indicated as *jñā*. *Jñā* means full of knowledge.

The word *purusha* has also been used to mean the individual soul. The question arises whether *purusha* is one or many. In this sūtra, the singular form of the word, designated by the suffix *-ah*, indicates that *purusha* is one, not many. In the *Sāmkhya Kārikā*, Īsvarakrsna describes pure spirit as *jñā*.[10] The knower is not indicated as *purusha*. *Jñā* is pure knower, pure consciousness, prior to becoming the indweller of all manifested forms and beings. *Purusha* means one who is residing or dwelling within a city. *Puri* means city or house. This physical body is a city with nine gates: two eyes, two ears, two nostrils, mouth, and two lower gates of procreation and elimination. When pure consciousness resides or indwells this physical body it is called *purusha*, but the pure form of this knower, which is above and beyond nature, is indicated as *jñā*.

Jñā is pure knowledge, pure consciousness, and it is distinctly separate from nature. When *jñā* dwells in the first projection of nature, and its qualities illuminate this medium of intellect, it is called *purusha*. The *Rig Veda* declares that one unborn *purusha* manifests in numerous forms. Consciousness cannot be divided. Anything with component parts is divisible, but something non-component cannot be divided. A country may claim sovereignty over its air space, but truly, no one can divide space. As space is indivisible so is consciousness, which is subtler than space. Krishna states that *purusha* is one—infinite and all-pervasive. "As the one sun illumines the entire world, so does the Lord of the field illumine the whole field."[11]

Purusha is one and is enlightening all *chittas* or intellects, and so we may wonder why all beings are not equally enlightened, or why all life spans are not the same. The Upanishads give an example of fire to explain how one *purusha* manifests in numerous forms. Fire is one, but it can manifest in

---

[9] *Bhagavad Gītā* XIII.17.
[10] *Sāmkhya Kārikā* II.
[11] *Bhagavad Gītā* XIII.33.

13

many forms at once. Fire disappears when its fuel has finished, and appears with new fuel. Manifestation and dissolution are going on always. Fire remains fire. From the *Katha Upanishad*, we read: "As fire is an all-pervasive power and can appear in numerous forms at the same time in numerous places, in the same way there is one consciousness, one *purusha*, manifesting in numerous places, in numerous forms."[12] *Purusha* manifests in many forms, not only in human form. It manifests in insects, reptiles, birds, and other animals. All living beings share consciousness. In the same way that fire manifests in many places, one *purusha* manifests through numerous *chittas*. *Chitta* is the medium for the manifestation of consciousness, and the number of *chittas* is countless.

The true nature of *purusha* is consciousness, knowledge, and eternal existence. It is all-pervasive. There is not any place where spirit does not dwell. *Purusha* enlightens all *chittas* or intellects, but its purity is beyond the intellect. One sun brings light to all creatures' eyes, but it exists above all eyes, and is not altered by any defect of the eye. In the same way, one *purusha* enlightens all minds, but it exists beyond the intellect and it is unaffected by any ignorance. Sāmkhya believes that bondage and emancipation are not related with *purusha* but with our intellect.

The individual soul, *jivātmā*, is not only *purusha*, but a combination of intellect and consciousness. The soul is individual due to the instrument or medium of manifestation, which is the intellect or *chitta*. That manifested form of *purusha* resides in our intellect. Pure consciousness is not called soul and it is not individual. The self of every being is supreme consciousness. Emancipation comes when we realize our own true nature as a manifestation of supreme consciousness, the guiding intelligence behind nature, and become one with that.

~~~

5
traigunyam
Three attributes:
sattva (light), *rajas* (movement), *tamas* (stability)

Kapila teaches that nature and spirit are the two root causes of this universe. First, he describes nature, *prakriti*, as one causal phenomenon having eight forms, which produces sixteen effects. He then teaches that

---

[12] *Katha Upanishad* II.2.9.

purusha is one all-pervasive consciousness indwelling and enlightening all intellects. Now he gives a description of the properties of nature— *traigunyam*, three *gunas*.

Guna means quality or attribute. *Sattva, rajas*, and *tamas* are the three attributes of nature or energy. Light is the quality of sattva, movement is the quality of *rajas*, and stability is the quality of *tamas*. The causal form of nature is called *sattoguna*. It is only radiance. This causal form is enlivened by *purusha*, which inspires movement and the radiance becomes active. This activity compounds energy into bundles of atoms. The movement is called *rajoguna*, and the formation of compounds is called *tamoguna*. *Rajoguna* is subtle form, and *tamoguna* is gross form.

These three attributes are the qualities of nature that cause nature to transform into effects and create forms. Forms are nothing but combined elements. When *purusha* enlivens the causal form of the intellect, the body takes shape. When the attractive power of *purusha* leaves the physical body, the compound elements forming the body merge back into their own root cause in energy.

Purusha is one and pervades all of nature. Spirit is present in every medium nature creates. *Purusha* is pure consciousness, and when it reflects into the media of nature, then life appears. All projections, except for the gross elements, reflect consciousness. The appearance of diverse forms is due to the attributes of nature, which cause all-pervasive spirit to appear as many.

This is similar to space within and outside of a container. Space is all-pervading and exists both in and out of all containers. It seems as if space is contained, but the container merely defines a boundary of space. We come to think of certain spaces as belonging to us, but we know that the earth rotates and orbits the sun, while the whole galaxy moves. Therefore the space inside our house and even inside our bodies is always changing. We have never existed in the same space for any length of time, yet we think we can contain and claim space.

Similarly, spirit or consciousness is all-pervading, and the limits and boundaries we experience are constructions of nature and its three attributes. We may believe that all-pervading consciousness, experienced as our individual consciousness, is specific to us. In reality we receive consciousness from one all-pervasive source. Just as we mistakenly define space by the boundaries we create, we define our existence by the boundaries of nature and impose limits on limitless spirit. Spirit does not simply reside in nature; it pervades nature. It is omnipresent and omniscient, and we owe our existence to the qualities of spirit.

The three *gunas* are enlivened by *purusha*, and the expressions of the *gunas* can be seen in every aspect of existence. They manifest at every level. The qualities of *sattoguna* are light, knowledge, wisdom, happiness, and an awakened, focused mind. When *sattoguna* prevails in our intellect, we experience pure wisdom, happiness, and divine feelings. But *sattva* is a *guna*, a property of nature and not the pure form of *purusha*. If we are attached in any way with any attribute, we will be bound to nature, and the cycle of birth and death will continue. Krishna states that all *gunas*, even *sattva*, bind the embodied one.[13]

The first projection of *rajoguna* is *ahamkāra*, ego. Ego is the active power, the doer. But when the ego becomes egoistic then desire and restlessness emerge, and after contact with the objects of senses, passion and infatuation increase. In the *Bhagavad Gītā*, *rajas* is characterized by passion arising from thirst and attachment, which "binds the embodied one."[14] When *rajoguna* prevails in the mind, we are not peaceful and our thoughts are scattered. We need *rajoguna* because without it we cannot function. All actions are related with *rajoguna*. But when *rajoguna* is dominant, greed, anger and other malevolent forces compel us toward harm. *Rajoguna* must work under the influence of *sattoguna* for our actions to be uplifting.

Krishna states that *tamoguna* is born of ignorance and confuses all embodied beings. It binds with negligence, indolence, and sleepiness.[15] Carelessness creates delusion and infatuation, bogging us down in ignorance. These are the qualities of *tamoguna*. And yet we need *tamoguna* to become embodied beings.

Tamoguna and *rajoguna* are both useful. Without *tamoguna* we would not exist in human form, and without *rajoguna* we could not act or do practice. In moderation and in the light of *sattoguna*, these two qualities are useful as we seek realization. All three *gunas* are part of nature, existing at all times. Their impact in our lives depends on which one is dominant.

~~~

---

[13] *Bhagavad Gītā* XIV.5.

[14] *Bhagavad Gītā* XIV.7.

[15] *Bhagavad Gītā* XIV.8.

Sāmkhya

6
sañcharah prati-sañcharah
Evolution and involution

Kapila now teaches that the three states of nature are involved in two processes: evolution and involution. The evolution of nature in twenty-four stages is called *sañcharah*. The first form of nature is unmanifest energy, which projects through twenty-three effects. *Prati-sañcharah*, involution, occurs when these effects merge back into unmanifest energy. In involution the effects return to their cause. At the level of unmanifest nature, there is complete dissolution back into the cause.

Evolution and involution are the actions of the three *gunas*. As a gas may become a liquid and then a solid, and then reverse this process and change from a solid to a liquid and back to gas, in the same way the three *gunas* emerge and merge back into the causal state. All things in nature are in a constant state of flux. The three *gunas* are never annihilated, but they appear in the process of evolution and become quiet in the process of involution. They exist eternally, proceeding from causal to subtle to gross and then receding from gross back through subtle to causal.

Scientists tell us that the causal phenomenon of this universe is energy. Energy evolves into matter and dissolves into energy. The sum total of energy is always the same. There is no increase or decrease. Energy is energy and, although it is beyond our vision, we know it exists because we see its effects.

Sāmkhya teaches that energy and consciousness are the source of existence. Sāmkhya reasons that nature is the material cause of this universe, but nature by itself is insentient. Therefore, nature, alone, cannot create a universe full of conscious intelligence. Sāmkhya says that neither nature nor spirit is the sole cause of this universe. They work together in the light of spirit. Evolution and involution are the expressions of nature. Evolution is the projection into forms and involution is dissolution, a return to the causal state.

In the Upanishads we read: "One unborn nature evolves many intellects, and that nature has three colors, white, red and black." [16] White refers to *sattoguna*, red stands for *rajoguna*, and *black* represents tamoguna. "That unborn nature produces numerous progeny according to her quality. She has three colors and all her progeny have three colors," meaning that

---

[16] *Svetāshvatara Upanishad* IV.5.

17

every intellect has all three attributes. "One unborn being enjoys that projection, and other unborn beings leave that when they have completed their own experience."[17] *Purusha* is separate from nature and eternally observes and enjoys nature. Individual beings develop through a process of evolution, gain experience, and become realized attaining emancipation. Nature is for both experience and emancipation. The projection of nature is a natural process, comprised of the *gunas* and inspired by consciousness, without beginning or end.

Nature evolves from causal to subtle to gross and then returns from gross to subtle to causal. The causal level is beyond our perception. The subtle is perceived and the gross is seen. There are three visible and two perceptible primordial elements. Earth, water and fire are visible. Air and space are perceptible. Our inner senses, the mind, ego, and intellect, are beyond perception and vision, but they can be realized.

In meditation, we work with the mind, ego, and intellect in a natural process of involution. Once our external efforts stop, the body and senses become quiet. As the activity of the mind and ego are observed, they gradually settle and rest in the intellect. The intellect works to discern the observer distinct from all activity. Gradually, the effort of the intellect stops and we can cross the limitation of nature and experience *purusha*.

The uniqueness of Sāmkhya is that it teaches us to practice with something that is accessible to us and gradually take our practice to a higher level. It is difficult to contemplate the unmanifest. Sāmkhya teaches us to start with what we know. We understand energy. Gradually as we analyze what we see, perceive, and realize, we begin to wonder, "Who is seeing and knowing?" In this process, we reach *purusha* as we realize that all forms of nature are changing, while *purusha*, our real self, is the unchanging observer of these changes. Nature provides the means for us to turn inward and realize that our real self is *purusha*.

This world, which is eternally coming and going, is a projection of a natural process. As the wind induces waves on the ocean, spirit inspires nature and evolves life as part of an eternal process of evolution and involution.

~~~

---

[17] *Ibid.*

7
adhyātmam adhibhūtam adhidaivam ca
Suffering due to self, other beings, and the divine world

Suffering is an aspect of the unfoldment of nature. *Adhyātma* is the suffering we create for ourselves in our intellects, minds, bodies and emotions. This category of affliction may be triggered by bad habits, our attachments to people and things, or our ignorance. *Adhibhūta* is the suffering caused by other worldly beings, from a very small virus to a large animal, or a powerful, abusive person. *Adhidaiva* is the misery from divine calamities, such as earthquakes or hurricanes. Regardless of what triggers our pain, our suffering may be visible and obvious or less apparent, but perceptible.

We cannot control divine calamities, and we cannot control what others will do to us, but we can take care of our own well-being. Physical disease is related with our wind, bile, and phlegm. When these substances act in balance, we are healthy. When they are out of balance, we become sick. When wind (*vāta*), bile (*pitta*), or phlegm (*kapha*) is out of proportion, numerous diseases appear. Imbalances may be caused by the air we breathe, the liquids we drink, or the food we eat. When we take food or drink to satisfy cravings rather than discerning what is useful for our health, we risk causing disease. Some foods act against each other. If they are eaten together, they disturb the body's balance. When balance is disturbed, diseases appear. Our external environment can also cause disease. For example, if the air we breathe is polluted, it can make us sick. When we eat nourishing food, drink what hydrates us, and breathe fresh, clean air, we support our good health.

Beyond physical disease is mental distress. Many of us suffer from misguided thinking, useless speculation and unfulfilled desire. Some mental illness can be temporarily subdued by medication, but the root cause of misery is not alleviated. Whenever we accumulate wealth, physical objects or relationships, the need to protect and preserve what we have arises. We do not want to lose what we have gained. This leads to an endless cycle of accumulation, fear, and loss. Everything in this world is constantly changing and loss is inevitable. Even if we could keep a cherished person or thing exactly as they are, our feelings of satisfaction are impermanent. Our ideas of what is important constantly change throughout our lives.

Even the attainment of heaven is temporary according to Sāmkhya. Heaven is not a permanent abode, but a transitory place earned according to our good actions. Our time in heaven ends when the results of our good actions expire and we must then return to the physical world. After death we maintain our state of mind at the time of death. If we uplift ourselves in our present life, we will enjoy upliftment. If we are full of ignorance and vice when our body dies, this misery continues. Infatuation and delusion are diseases of the intellect, and the root of all other diseases. *Ayurveda* teaches that ignorance is the source of all illness. Even bad eating habits arise from a mistake of intellect. Not eating properly indicates a lack of wisdom. Many kinds of mental diseases appear because the intellect is not guiding the mind. In the Upanishads we read that the mind and senses are under the guidance of the intellect.[18] If the intellect is weak and polluted, it does not provide good leadership for the mind and senses. When the intellect is contaminated by delusions and the infatuation of the ego, it loses the power of pure wisdom.

Intellectual disease is more dangerous than mental disease. Fanaticism is an intellectual disease and wars are caused by this kind of pollution. Many powerful people have killed vast populations because they did not conform to some fundamentalist thought or arbitrary standard. This kind of disease is not generally curable because fanatics and fundamentalists do not want to listen to reason. Throughout history, millions of people have been killed due to intellectual disease. Intellectual disease appears as mental illness in the form of greed, passion, infatuation, delusion, and illusion. The cause of these symptoms is our disturbed thoughts.

Adhibhūta is suffering related with worldly affairs, and comes from our interactions with other beings. Regardless of what kind of life we lead, we may be preyed upon. There are dangerous beasts, reptiles, insects, viruses and germs. We may be healthy and strong, but a tiny mosquito can give us malaria. Other people may make us the target of a scheme or cruelty. Numerous kinds of suffering come from other beings.

The final category is *adhidaiva*, the suffering caused by the elements. The divine powers of earth, water, fire, and wind bring earthquakes, floods, fires, and strong winds. The natural elements are divine because they give equally to all. Fire gives warmth to all beings, yet it can also bring disaster. Water is essential for life, but it can be mightily destructive. The divine

---

[18] The *Katha Upanishad* I.3.3-9, uses an analogy of a chariot.

elements are powerful forces and *adhidaivika* suffering is caused by these forces that are beyond our control.

The goal of Sāmkhya philosophy is the permanent removal of suffering. If a cause exists in our lives, then the effects of that cause will naturally come into our lives. Nature's unfoldment is not the cause of our suffering. We suffer because we identify with the limited forms of nature. We are a manifestation of *purusha*, which is infinite, pure consciousness, above the three attributes and beyond nature's unfoldment. When we realize this truth, we are freed from suffering. When we understand our true nature in consciousness, there is no place for suffering. Until that realization, we are ultimately the cause of our own suffering, whether pain comes into our lives from our own behavior, other beings, or the great forces of nature. As long as we continue in the cycle of birth and death, we are subjected to pain. Freedom from suffering is found by realizing our real identity as the knower, *purusha*.

We begin our search for this freedom by comprehending nature and its qualities, the three *gunas*. Patañjali states: "The seen, which has the three attributes of light, movement and stability, manifests in the form of elements and senses and is for experience and emancipation."[19] The *gunas* are always moving throughout this projected world, providing us with experiences, both good and bad. We must use this opportunity to learn and use our faculties for realizing truth. This is how we become freed from misery. Ironically, if we use our human faculties to chase enjoyment and run from suffering, we will never be free of suffering.

~~~

8
pañcha abhi-buddhayah
Five sources of knowledge:
intellect, ego, mind, five cognitive senses and five active senses

We have five sources of knowledge that should be used to realize truth. In fact, everything we do is related with these five sources of knowledge. The five sources begin with the intellect, which appears in the form of the ego. The ego appears in the form of the mind, and the mind perceives through the activities of the five perceptive senses and five active senses.

---

[19] *Yoga Sūtras* II-18.

The intellect, ego, mind, five senses, and five organs of action are the means for experiencing the world and gaining knowledge.

These thirteen of the twenty-four aspects of nature are the sources for acquiring knowledge. The other eleven aspects of nature—the five primordial elements, five subtle elements, and causal nature—are the objects of knowledge. There is only one subject, *purusha*, which is knowledge itself.

The *Katha Upanishad* says our active senses face out toward this universe, rather than in toward the internal world. We can see things outside ourselves, but we do not see what is inside.[20] Our eyes see stars from millions of miles away but do not see what is behind the retina. The power of sight faces outward. The same goes for all of our cognitive senses; their powers of perception are external. Our active senses include the mouth for eating and speaking, the hands for handling, the legs for traveling, the organs of procreation for reproduction, and the organs of elimination for excreting. All of these help us function in the external world. Our mind and ego also focus on the world outside the body. Even the intellect remains busy with our worldly affairs, and does not recognize spirit's illuminating power.

When a person finds freedom through an understanding of nature and the knowledge of spirit, he or she lives in the true self. This is the only abiding, blissful, painless state. "When the self is one with *Brahman*, the self enjoys imperishable bliss."[21]

~~~

9
pañcha karma-yonayah
Five causes of action:
evidence, fallacy, fancy, sleep, memory

All actions leave their impressions, and these impressions may spur us on toward knowledge or lead us away from the truth. The five causes of action are evidence or proof, fallacy, fancy, sleep, and recollection or memory.[22]

---

[20] *Katha Upanishad* II.1.1
[21] *Bhagavd Gītā* V.21.
[22] See also *Yoga Sūtras* I-5 through 11.

Proof comes in three forms: perception or visual evidence, inference, and testimony from a trustworthy source. The need to realize and know truth inspires us to activate our search.

Fallacy is the ignorance of accepting the body as the soul. Most of us buy into some level of this fallacy by thinking that this changing, impure body is most dear to us, placing it on the level of the eternal soul.[23] If we accept this fundamental fallacy, we create misery for ourselves as we try to establish lasting happiness in the impermanent body and senses. We do not see reality and we live in misidentification. The Sanskrit word, *viparyaya*, translates as "against the truth." Fallacy is the opposite of knowledge. We believe in a fallacy in spite of evidence of the truth. The result of fallacy is that we believe the body is our real self. If our body is weak, we think we are weak. If the body is healthy, we think we are strong. Our sense of self becomes defined by this transitory, impure body. Even the most beautiful, healthy body has impurities, such as excrement or decay. Only the soul remains completely pure within the body. When the soul departs from the body, the body decomposes.

The third cause of action is fancy, an imagined conceptualization of life. This can manifest as paranoia, delusions, phobias or fantasies. Most of us spend much of our lives dreaming of the future or re-imagining the past. We create fanciful stories that distort reality. Even while sleeping and dreaming, our memories are related with either fallacy or fancy.

Sleep is the state for restoring the energy we expended. When we are exhausted, we enter into deep sleep and re-energize. We must rest to restore our energy, and we must work to sustain ourselves. But we should keep a balance between work and rest.

The fifth cause of action is memory. Our memory serves us from day to day, allowing us to continue our work. And this memory travels with us from lifetime to lifetime. Memory is a powerful resource as we seek the truth.

~~~

---

[23] *Yoga Sūtras* II-5.

10
pañcha vāyavah
Five winds:
prāna, apāna, samāna, vyāna, udāna

There are five kinds of breath in our body. These five *vāyus* enliven the body and give us the power for action. *Prana* governs the area from the nostrils to the heart; *apāna* travels from the navel to the toes; *samāna* goes from the heart to the navel; *vyāna* pervades the whole body; and *udāna* moves in the area from the thyroid to the top of the head.

Prāna	Upward Moving
Apāna	Downward Moving
Samāna	Central
Vyāna	Spreading Energy
Udāna	Head

Prāna moves through the mouth and nose. *Prāna* provides the power to purify our blood, giving energy to the heart, lungs, and thyroid. *Apāna* moves energy away from the upper body. "*A*" means away from. *Samāna* resides in the center of the body, feeding the gastric fire and aiding digestion. *Udāna* carries energy up. It inspires the cognitive senses and brain. *Vyāna* pervades the whole body. It provides energy to the body through the circulatory and nervous systems

Pure consciousness manifests in the intellect and initiates two kinds of movement: thought and breath. Thought is the result of consciousness and breath is the result of energy. We receive energy and discharge toxins through breath. Because of this process, breath is the root of our bodily existence, allowing us to be alive in a functioning body, but Kapila explains that breath is not the cause of life. It is the effect of an illumined intellect.

The span of our life is based on our breath. We lose our precious breath by expending energy unnecessarily. Passion, anger, fear, and greed lead to uncontrolled breathing causing us to lose our breath. If we control our breath when we exert ourselves, then energy is not wasted, but if our breath is uncontrolled from over-exertion or unrestrained emotions, we waste energy and shorten our lifespan.

~~~

11
pañcha karma-ātmānah
Five essences of action:
self-restraint, practice, dispassion, stable intellect, wisdom

Kapila states there are five actions that support the development and achievement of a pure intellect. A pure intellect enables us to fulfill the purpose of our human life, which is to realize the self. The five actions are: self-restraint, practice, dispassion, stable intellect, and wisdom: *yama*, *abhyāsa*, *vairāgya*, *samādhi*, and *prajñā*.

The primary essence of practice is self-restraint, *yama*,[24] and it has five limbs. The first three limbs are non-violence, truthfulness, and non-stealing. Many great spiritual leaders have taught us how to live according to these truths. As we observe ourselves in relationship with others, we create a platform for spiritual upliftment.

The fourth *yama* is *brahmacharya*, often translated as celibacy, abstinence from using sexual energy. Here *brahmacharya* means controlling our emotions. *Brahmacharya* emphasizes the mindful use of our energy in relationship with others.

The fifth *yama* is non-accumulation. When we accumulate more than we need, we are hoarding what others could use. By doing this, we deny the rights of others. There are always people who have a majority of the wealth. The advantages of this world are not just for a few people. Everyone has a right to use the world's resources judiciously, but some people hoard, while others have nothing. The gap between rich and poor is created by unethical accumulation.

In the *Śrīmad Bhāgavatam*,[25] Narada teaches: "Human beings have the right to fill their stomachs. If they accumulate more than that they are thieves, snatching the rights of others." Filling the stomach means taking care of needs. This includes saving for the future and the careful use of resources. There is a great difference between need and desire, or necessity and greed. Necessity is undeniable, but desire is unreasonable. We all want to live happy lives and fulfill our needs, but unrestrained accumulation is harmful. Non-accumulation and the control of energy are central to non-stealing, truthfulness, and non-violence. All five are the foundation of an ethical and spiritual life.

---

[24] See also *Yoga Sūtras* II-35 through 39.
[25] An epic story on *bhakti yoga* (devotion) by Vyasdev.

The second essence of action is the practice of meditation, *abhyāsa*.[26] *Abhyāsa* means to think again and again upon the source of self, to repeatedly place our minds on the source of our consciousness.

Dispassion is *vairāgya*.[27] *Rāga* is passion, desire, and *vairāgya* is evenness. Dispassion is non-attachment. Through practice we turn toward the source of our own self for fulfillment, and no longer identify with the objects of nature. There are two categories of objects that create temptation: visible objects of enjoyment, and perceptible concepts, such as ideas of heaven and subtle powers. *Vairāgya* is letting go of our need to form identity outside the self.

The fourth essence of action is stable intellect, *samādhi*. There are four levels of *samādhi*: concentration, contemplation, meditation, and complete absorption into the source. In concentration we focus our minds. In contemplation, we bring the mind away from distractions, returning again and again to our point of focus. In meditation, we experience unwavering awareness. And in complete absorption, we realize oneness, *samādhi*.[28]

The *Yoga Sūtras* discuss three stages: *dhāranā*, *dhyāna*, and *samādhi*. In *dhāranā*, we create a one-pointed focus and repeatedly return to this focus when the mind wanders off. In *dhyāna*, contemplation and meditation are combined. The mind finds a steady, quiet internal focus and merges back into the ego. As the ego quiets, it merges back toward its source in the intellect. In *samādhi*, the intellect is stable; there is complete absorption of our identity into its source. At this stage the intellect is unmoving. *Samādhi* is evenness of the intellect.

The final essence of action is stable wisdom, *prajñā*.[29] Stable wisdom comes through *samādhi*. The *Bhagavad Gītā* states: "That wisdom stands firm in one whose senses are withdrawn from the objects of senses."[30] In this state, the intellect is stable, and clear discrimination between the self and the object occurs. *Prajñā* is the wisdom that arises in a pure and stable intellect.

The essences of action are related with our development and upliftment. They help us to release our attachments and develop clear discrimination, lifting us above the *gunas* of nature, and freeing us from

---

[26] See also *Yoga Sūtras* I-13.

[27] See also *Yoga Sūtras* I-15.

[28] See also *Yoga Sūtras* III-1.

[29] See also *Yoga Sūtras* I-48 and 49.

[30] *Bhagavad Gītā* II.68.

suffering. The *Bhagavad Gītā* declares that action is an individual's creative power.[31] If we devote our resources, including energy, ability, breath, and time, to these five actions, our actions will uplift us. Effort is required.

~ ~ ~

12
pañcha-parvāh avidyāh
Five knots of false knowledge:
darkness, infatuation, great infatuation, aversion, blind aversion

The five knots of false knowledge begin with ignorance and they are bound securely by the fear of loss or death. Patañjali presents this same idea but uses different terms. In the *Yoga Sūtras* the five knots are called *kleśas*, miseries.[32] Once the initial darkness or ignorance is present the other four knots or miseries spring forth.

Kapila's Five Knots		Patañjali's Miseries	
Tama	Darkness	*Avidyā*	Ignorance
Moha	Infatuation	*Asmitā*	Egoism
Mahāmoha	Great infatuation	*Rāga*	Attraction
Tāmisra	Aversion	*Dvesa*	Aversion
Andha-tāmisra	Blind aversion	*Abhiniveśa*	Fear of death

In the first stage of ignorance, *avidyā*, our intellect is covered by *tamoguna*, darkness. When we are ignorant, the intellect does not discriminate between what is real and what is unreal. With this lack of discernment, we do not recognize how two distinct powers are present forming our life. We blend the qualities of *purusha* with the individual medium of intellect and think "I-am, I am intelligent, I exist." The qualities of intelligence and existence are attributed to the intellect rather than to spirit. In this way we form a state of existence and awareness separate

---

[31] *Bhagavad Gītā* VIII.3.
[32] See also *Yoga Sūtras* II-3 through 9.

from a unified state of consciousness. This state is called infatuation or egoism, *asmitā*.

From egoism, our infatuation grows into attachment, great infatuation. *Moha* means infatuation, and *maha* means "great." When we are infatuated, the ego faces outward and experience gained outside the self becomes the source of our identity. We identify with whatever gives us pleasure, the great infatuation. Inevitably, this outward seeking brings us pain, which gives rise to aversion.

As we experience pleasure and then attachment, passion appears. We want more of what we enjoy, and we become angry if we are thwarted. As we try to protect what we like and reject what we dislike, fear, hatred, greed and jealousy arise. Attraction and aversion are inevitable when we identify with experience.

Our strongest aversion is the fear of loss, *abhiniveśa*. This is the final knot, blind aversion. Mortality stirs up the greatest fear of humankind. We are afraid of death because we do not want to lose ourselves, but death is related with the body, not with *purusha*. This fear arises from our misidentification with the gross body.

All suffering can be traced to one of these five knots. If we live in ignorance of our true nature, we will always be caught in suffering, and we will be afraid of death. Kapila teaches that awareness alone will protect us from the pain of false knowledge. If we want to be happy, we must reduce *tamoguna* and egoism, and then work to remove passion and its companions, jealousy and hatred. Gradually we untie the five knots and move toward freedom.

Patañjali states that ignorance is the root of suffering and gives rise to the other four *kleśas*.[33] Likewise, Sāmkhya teaches that only the light of pure wisdom brings lasting bliss. Without discriminative knowledge, we will not be happy. Without wisdom, we identify with the projection of nature and we suffer. In ignorance, we identify with the physical world, believing that we are our bodies, senses, minds, and egos. Our possessiveness, our thinking in terms of "me" and "mine," must be replaced with pure knowledge, pure wisdom and understanding.

From the intellect to the body, we are projections of nature. We cannot claim that anything belongs to us. Every effect belongs to its cause,

---

[33] *Yoga Sūtras* II-4.

28

and every effect merges back into its cause. When the body dies, it merges into its own cause, the primordial elements.

Nature is the cause of body. Physically, mentally, and intellectually we become attached to our bodies, but these instruments are effects of nature. Spirit enlightens these instruments. Everything we can name belongs to nature and will one day merge back into nature. Nature changes and is never permanent in any form. Because of attachment, we wish to control our world and our experiences. When things are the way we like them, we hope to prevent change, but change is an unavoidable principle of nature.

According to Sāmkhya, when we realize truth, the ego continues to exist in the light of wisdom but it is no longer a cause of bondage. The ego becomes an instrument, a servant of higher wisdom. As long as we are knotted up with false knowledge, we suffer from ignorance, attachment, neediness, vice, hatred and fear. When we realize the highest truth, all instruments, including the ego and the mind, are transformed. The faculties remain, but they are guided by pure wisdom, virtue, knowledge, and detachment. In the light of wisdom we are free from bondage and suffering.

~~~

13
astāvimśati-dhā aśaktih
Twenty-eight kinds of weakness

There are twenty-eight limitations related with the sources of gaining discriminative knowledge. Eleven are related to defects in the eleven organs: the five perceptive senses, the five active senses, and the mind. Nine are related with ego satisfaction—the ability to meet our desires and complacency with the pleasure attained. And eight relate with perfection of the intellect—the lack of these gifts makes the path more challenging. Ego satisfaction is discussed in *sūtra* 14 and the gifts which help practice are discussed in *sūtra* 15.

The deficiencies of the eleven organs are: deafness, blindness, paralysis, loss of taste, loss of smell, muteness, impairment of hands or legs, constipation, impotence and insanity.

Our practice is related with our senses, mind, ego, and intellect. If any of these thirteen means are restricted, our capacity is limited. Without developed instruments our ability to gain knowledge is stunted. If we are blind, we can realize truth in other ways besides sight, but it is impossible

29

to know this material world completely. We have countless lifetimes to work toward our goal, and each lifetime brings different circumstances. We must take advantage of the capacity we have in this life and move toward truth.

~~~

14
navadhā tuśtih
Nine-fold satisfactions:
cognitive senses, nature, time, means and luck

Nine kinds of contentment limit our spiritual progress and delay our attainment of knowledge. The ego accepts or rejects experience, and becomes satisfied or dissatisfied. Therefore, these nine-fold satisfactions are related with ego. Generally, if we are satisfied with the way things are, we become complacent and will not search for higher truth.

The first five satisfactions correspond to the enjoyment of the five objects of the senses. When the cognitive senses demand stimulation, we cannot focus internally. If our senses are gratified, we may be deluded into thinking there is no other source of happiness. When the five senses are satisfied with the objects of the senses, the need to seek is lulled by satiation. This sets us up for suffering. Aging, injury or changing circumstances diminish our capacity to enjoy sensory pleasures. All of nature is transitory, including our faculties. When we lose our faculties or lose the ability to gather objects we suffer.

The four remaining satisfactions are nature, time, means, and luck. These are related with our commitment to seek knowledge. We may believe in nature, observing that nature has been merciful and kind, providing us with instruments and raising us from lower life forms to this human form without our effort. And so we believe that nature will continue to work and carry us to perfection and emancipation.

Then there are those individuals who have gained the means for spiritual progress. They receive initiation and instruction from a guru, and believe their upliftment is the guru's responsibility, and the guru's grace is all that is needed. They may believe that when they die the guru will lift their souls to a higher place. They may even feel that they are elevated to the guru's level by being in their guru's presence. Our study with a guru should inspire us, rather than make us complacent.

Many people are waiting for an auspicious time to gain knowledge and do spiritual practices. We may wait for a special moment to arise when all the right conditions are present before beginning our search. Now, we may tell ourselves, we are too busy, too tired, or having too much fun to think about self and the source of self. We do not realize the right time to begin is always now.

Perhaps we believe that fate or luck will determine our chance for emancipation. Why concern ourselves or make an effort? It is out of our hands. This is a mistake. Good fortune is the result of our previous *karma*. Luck is not by chance—it is the result of our previous actions. Our work yesterday becomes our luck today. Our efforts today determine our luck tomorrow. If we think it is up to luck to realize truth, we must understand the source of good fortune and begin to seek the truth.

Practice is essential in the search for ultimate truth. Again and again, we must practice controlling the senses, controlling the mind, and making our wisdom pure. In the *Katha Upanishad* we find: "When these five cognitive senses stop their movement and are free from their own objects, then the mind will be stable, the intellect will be unmoving, and there will be no projection of egoism. That is the highest state, *samādhi*, and in that state one can realize truth, not before that."[34]

~~~

15

asta-dhā siddhih
Eight gifts or perfections:
a lack of the gifts of wisdom, sound, study, divine grace, service, and a lack of freedom from the three kinds of suffering

Knowledge is the path to remove ignorance and bondage. The process for gaining knowledge begins as we think about life, its cause, and why we are suffering. We use our reasoning and logic and our quest begins. We study some scriptures to guide our thinking. In studying, many questions arise and we seek a teacher to help with our understanding.

This guide or guru shares knowledge and truth. A worthy and compassionate teacher offers us a deeper insight into truth. With knowledge and practice, suffering begins to lift from our lives and we move toward emancipation. The eight gifts are related with this process.

---

[34] *Katha Upanishad* II.3.10.

Kapila's eight kinds of *siddhis*, perfections, are different from those given by Patañjali in the *Yoga Sutras*.[35] The *siddhis* described by Patañjali are *yogic* states of achievement that may create hindrances on the path. Through challenging practices, a person may achieve unusual powers and gain status without necessarily becoming realized. It is not uncommon for a watchful teacher to rein in a student's emphasis on the development of the *siddhis* because they are a great distraction from higher practice.

In Sāmkhya there are eight perfections or gifts related with the intellect. The lack of any of these deters us from treading firmly on the path. The first gift a practitioner achieves is wisdom and the power of discrimination. If we have practiced and gained wisdom in a previous life, our progress is carried into this life.[36] Special qualities come from previous action, and wisdom comes from prior practice. One might say that different qualities arise from different combinations of DNA, but Sāmkhya teaches that we have had previous lives, and qualities are developed through previous experience. Transmigration of the subtle body is a process of evolution. Scientists accept the theory of evolution, from the single-cellular amoeba to the development of the human form. The evolution of the enlivened medium through different forms of life is a principle of Sāmkhya.

If our car breaks down on a journey, we do not return to begin the journey again. We repair the car and continue from where we are. Whatever part of the journey has been completed remains so. The same is true in our spiritual development. The practice we have established is retained as we resume our practice in the next life from where we left off. We do not lose the fruit of practice. Working to achieve higher consciousness and pure wisdom expands our capacity to realize truth. The discriminative power of wisdom is a blessing, and without it our search for truth is debilitated.

---

[35] Patañjali's *siddhis* are *animā, mahimā, garimā, laghimā, prāpti, prākāmya, īsitva,* and *vasitva. Animā* is becoming minute. *Mahimā* is the opposite, the power to come into a large form. *Laghimā* is the ability to become as light as a feather, and *garimā* is the opposite, becoming heavy. *Prāpti* allows a person to get whatever object is desired. *Prākāmya* provides the power to do whatever one likes. *Īsitva* is the divine power to reign over the three worlds. And *Vasitva* is the power to bring anything under one's control.

[36] See also *Yoga Sutras* I-19.

The second gift is sound. A *mantra* transmits energy and divine power through sound. The sound of *mantra* assists the elevation of our awareness. Traditionally, a *mantra* is given by a guru to a disciple.

The third gift is the study of scriptures from which we glean divine teachings, a divine path, and divine truth. We can gain knowledge through the study of worthy texts.

The fourth gift is the divine grace of a great *yogi* or guru. A guru can give us a *mantra* and share wisdom. As we recite our *mantra* with discernment, study and practice, we become worthy of our guru's grace, which guides us toward absolute truth and the end of suffering.

Some of us are able to serve wise teachers. Our capacity to serve is one of the gifts or perfections. Through service, we are able to gain knowledge.

These five gifts are helpful in enhancing our practice and establishing our identity above the transformations of nature. A lack of any one of these gifts diminishes our capacity to practice. When we are established in *purusha*, nature will still change and the three kinds of suffering presented in *sutra* 7 will still exist, but we will not suffer a loss of self-identity because our ignorance will be removed. *Adhyātma,* the pain caused by our own ignorance, will diminish with proper choices. *Adhidaiva* is pain caused by the elements, which we can only accept and grieve. And with compassion we learn to manage and tolerate the suffering that comes from the ignorance of other beings, *adhibhūta.*

Among all the animals, the one who causes the most suffering is man. One human being can cause the suffering of millions through sweeping destruction, including pollution, genocide, bombings and war. Knowledge frees us of attachment. Attachment to the world is the cause of suffering. The outward causes of pain will continue, but the one who is free can rise above suffering.

~~~

16
daśa mūlika-arthāh
Ten primary qualities

Sāmkhya explains that this universe is a projection of nature and spirit. There are ten fundamental qualities ascribed to nature and/or spirit as they manifest in form. Four describe both nature and spirit, three refer to the projection of nature, and three describe the unique status of the individual soul. This enumeration provides clarity about the manifested world and a basis for discrimination when searching for truth.

The four qualities that belong to both nature and spirit are *astitva*, *sanyoga*, *viyoga*, and *sesvrititva*: principal existence, union, disunion, and finite existence, respectively. Anything that projects into life exists because of nature and spirit. All forms result from the union of nature and spirit. Nature and spirit can be separated back into their original state. And everything in existence is finite.

Qualities Belonging to Both Nature and Spirit	
Astitva	Principal existence
Sanyoga	Union
Viyoga	Disunion
Sesvrititva	Finite existence

The first principle, *astitva*, affirms that everything in existence has two primary causes: nature and spirit. Both are eternal. The *Bhagavad Gītā* states that whatever is seen in visible form is a projection of both the field (nature) and the knower of the field (spirit).[37] Nature alone cannot project. Spirit alone cannot take form.

Life manifests from invisible energy. Scientists document the existence of energy based on the effects of energy. They describe energy as weightless, colorless, formless, and limitless. All of these adjectives apply to causal energy. Like energy, consciousness is invisible. Nature and spirit must join together to appear in visible form. Form depends on the principal existence of both nature and spirit. Nature cannot project without spirit, and without nature there is no material cause for manifestation.

The second primary property is *sanyoga*, union.[38] Kapila indicates that everything in existence is the result of the union of spirit and nature. It is the co-existence of these two that produces all forms.

Sanyoga means the union of two. Often *yoga* is translated as union, but this is not the correct meaning. *Yoga* means to yoke, merge, or to be one.

---

[37] *Bhagavad Gītā* XIII.26.
[38] See also *Yoga Sūtras* II-23.

Samkhya

Nature and spirit join together and form a union, but they remain distinct, they do not become one. Two similar entities merging into oneness is *yoga*. When a river flows into a lake, that is called *yoga*. Water merges into water and becomes one. Once the river water flows into the lake water, the river water cannot be separated back out—the two become one. But if we put oil into water, these two can be separated because they have different qualities. Combining oil with water is *sanyoga*.

The third property shared by nature and spirit is *viyoga*, separation. When two distinct things have been joined together, they can be separated back into two. Everything in existence arises from changeable nature and changeless spirit. Nature and spirit are distinctly unique and they can be separated. Krishna declares, "Let the dissolution of union with pain be known as *yoga*."[39] When we separate our identity from nature, then we realize oneness with the spirit. This is *yoga*.

In the *Yoga Sūtras*, Patañjali teaches: "In the state of experience, as opposed to emancipation, there is no distinguishing between nature and the self (*purusha*). In truth they are absolutely unmixed." Nature and spirit are distinctly separate. They can never be united in any state, even though they appear to be united.[40] Patañjali gives an example to illumine this principle.[41] If you put a red flower near a crystal, then redness reflects in the crystal. The flower is separate and the crystal is separate, and if we look carefully, we see that the red color appears in the crystal because it reflects through the crystal. In the same way, spirit is not in nature: when nature becomes enlightened it looks as if spirit is in nature. Spirit is never one with nature because it has separate qualities. Spirit is the formless all-pervasive power that reflects in the intellect, making it appear that the two are united.

The final primary property of both nature and spirit is finite existence, *sesvrititva*. All forms are limited and finite. Energy and spirit are infinite, but when they project into diverse forms, the forms projected by their union are finite. Finite existence projects from the alliance of nature and spirit.

These are the four qualities related with both nature and spirit: all visible and perceptible forms exist due to the two principal causes of nature and spirit; manifestation is the result of nature and spirit's union;

[39] *Bhagavad Gītā* VI.23.
[40] *Yoga Sūtras* III-35.
[41] *Yoga Sūtras* I-41.

35

these two can be separated; and manifestation is finite. According to Sāmkhya, truth exists in the same form always, and untruth is changeable. Untruth does not deny existence; it is a term that indicates impermanence. Therefore, spirit is truth, and nature is untruth.

Of the remaining six qualities, three describe nature and three describe spirit. These primary qualities of nature or spirit indicate their essential properties. For instance, although nature appears as many, it is one in causal form. Therefore, oneness is a principle of nature. The cause of nature's projection into numerous forms is the presence of spirit. Contrary to what we might expect, plurality belongs to spirit because it inspires nature into diversity. In manifestation, spirit assumes the appearance of plurality because its all-pervasive power indwells as each individual soul.

Qualities of Nature	
Ekātattva	Oneness
Arthavatva	Purpose
Parārthya	Exists for others

Ekātattva, *arthavatva*, and *parārthya* are related with nature. Energy is one, serves a purpose, and exists for *purusha*. Oneness here refers to the oneness of energy in causal form. Although energy appears diverse in manifestation, all diversity comes from and remains one power of energy.

Spirit uses energy to appear in the form of cosmic and individual soul. This is the purpose of energy. Energy is the means by which forms appear and by which we can realize truth. Nature cannot produce anything without the light of spirit, but spirit has no capacity to produce anything. Nature's projection occurs with spirit's inspiration, and the purpose of manifestation is to convey and serve spirit.

Nature exists for *purusha*. Nature does not enjoy this manifestation. The river does not drink water. The fruit tree does not eat fruit. The earth produces wheat, but not for its own consumption. No natural projection is for nature; all manifestation serves spirit. Spirit enjoys nature and gains experience. All experience is related with knowledge, or consciousness.[42] *Purusha* is sentient, while nature is insentient. Nature is not aware of

---

[42] *Yoga Sūtras* II-18. "The dual purpose of nature is for experience and emancipation." Emancipation comes with knowledge of the real self as the seer.

knowledge. The body does not experience life, but the soul gains experience through the body. The body exists for spirit. As the body is the vehicle for the soul, nature is for *purusha*. Nature exists for spirit.

Qualities of Spirit	
Anyata	Separate from energy
Bahūtva	Plurality
Akartritva	Non-doer

Anyata, *bahūtva*, and *akartritva* are properties of *purusha*. Nature and spirit both have qualities that are distinct. When *purusha* appears as the indweller, it retains the properties of spirit. The quality of separation indicates that *purusha* remains separate from energy in manifestation. Consciousness is distinct from energy. Spirit manifests in diversity, inspiring everything in existence. Plurality is the second quality. And finally, spirit is the enjoyer of this plurality, not the doer. All movement and production are properties of nature. Action belongs to nature, in the light of spirit's awareness and observation. Defining spirit as the non-doer is the third quality of *purusha*.

Although they are synergists, spirit and nature remain unmixed. *Purusha* does not mingle with nature; it pervades and dwells within and without every medium, just as space dwells within and without a building. Buildings appear to divide space, but space is indivisible. Likewise, *purusha*'s properties are residing in every living form, appearing in plurality. Even though its appearance is plural, spirit remains one. In the *Bhagavad Gītā*, Krishna states: "Though spirit is one, spirit looks like many in different forms."[43] *Purusha* becomes as if many, as nature projects into different names and forms. This manifestation of plurality occurs in the diversity of nature. *Purusha* is one, indivisible consciousness. Plurality describes how consciousness appears in projection. And *purusha* is the enlightener and observer of nature's movement.

Sāmkhya philosophers teach that nature projects when inspired by consciousness. Both are eternal, but nature works in the light of spirit. *Purusha*, a sentient power, inspires insentient nature, and only then can nature's energy project into form.

---

[43] *Bhagavad Gītā* XIII.16.

Albert Einstein said that the universe inspires awe. We cannot help but feel some great power enlivens it. Spirit animates the manifestation of inanimate energy. The body works and moves. The senses receive information about the objects of the senses. The mind thinks. The intellect decides. All these activities function in our bodies in the light of spirit. Without spirit, there is no action or existence. The body works in the light of consciousness, and all of nature works in the light of spirit.

With knowledge and awareness, we realize that we are not the doer. Spirit enlightens and nature moves. *Purusha* is only seer; pure consciousness; one without a second; beyond the *gunas*, the three attributes of nature. In the *Bhagavad Gītā* we read: "Due to egoism, a deluded person believes that he or she is the doer. He or she is not the doer because all actions are going on in nature."[44]

The body, senses, mind, ego, and intellect are all projections of nature, not spirit. The real self, spirit, is not the doer, but due to egoism and infatuation, we believe we are the doer. Our ego is a projection of the intellect; and that ego takes ownership of action. All thoughts and activities start from the place where ego sprouts from intellect. In deep sleep, we lose this sense of doership and our sense of separate existence. But when we awaken, the ego reappears. We look around and think, "I will do this, I did that, and this is mine." Egoism is the root of doership and possessiveness, which cause suffering. *Purusha* is not the agent, not the doer. We limit our realization of consciousness by assuming doership.

The ten qualities of nature and spirit operate in the manifested world. Everything in this world can be traced to these ten primary qualities. We can realize the real self through unequivocal comprehension of these primary properties of nature and spirit.

~~~

17
anu-grahah sargah
Emanation is accumulation

Sargah is emanation or manifestation. Emanation, the production of form, is the result of accumulation, *anu-grahah*. The word *anu-grahah* has two roots: *anu* meaning many things are gathered, and *grahah* meaning

---

[44] *Bhagavad Gītā* III.27.

holding. Accumulation occurs when many things are held together in one place.

According to Sāmkhya, nature is the material cause of manifestation, whereby all phenomena are caused by the transformation and modifications of the three *gunas*. These three attributes modify into subtle elements, which produce the gross elements. Gross forms are constituted by a combination of five gross elements: space, air, heat, water and earth.

The elements have separate qualities and do not readily hold together. This is a wonder of nature. Think deeply and appreciate how great a wonder the body is. The elements combine, though their differing properties would keep them separate. The flames of a fire always go up. Water always flows down. One element rises and one descends. Air moves in all directions. Earth settles. All the elements are different, yet they combine in the living system of the body. In every manifestation within this universe, we find the same five elements. This combination of moving forces makes existence in visible form possible. This is *anu-grahah sargah*.

All gross objects are formed by the combination of universal gross elements, which are interchangeable in different forms. These gross elements are also called universal elements because they are universal properties available to all forms. Although the form appears to be consistent, there is constant migratory action among these universal elements. Every form is in a state of transition, even more so in complex forms, such as movable objects, which include our human form.

On a daily basis, our active senses interact with the material world as we breathe fresh air, drink water and eat food to maintain the body. We exchange old elements for new ones and eliminate the waste. Our human form is intimately connected with these universal properties.

Modern science uses different terminology for these universal particles, but in essence the idea is the same. There are universal particles or atoms used as building blocks to create forms. These particles assemble for a period of time and then move off to join in creating other forms. In *A Short History of Nearly Everything*, Bill Bryson summarizes the formation of one's human form according to modern science. Although he does not highlight the daily interchange of these particles he does summarize form as constituting existence and its disassembly as non-existence.

To begin with, for you to be here now trillions of drifting atoms had somehow to assemble in an intricate and intriguingly obliging manner to create you. It's an arrangement so specialized and particular that it has never been tried before and will only exist this once. For the next many years (we hope) these tiny particles will uncomplainingly engage in all the billions of deft, cooperative efforts necessary to keep you intact and let you experience the supremely agreeable but generally underappreciated state known as existence.

Why atoms take this trouble is a bit of a puzzle. Being you is not a gratifying experience at the atomic level. For all their devoted attention, your atoms don't actually care about you—indeed; don't even know that you are there. They don't even know that they are there. They are mindless particles, after all, and not even themselves alive. (It is a slightly arresting notion that if you were to pick yourself apart with tweezers, one atom at a time, you would produce a mound of fine atomic dust, nothing of which had ever been alive but all of which had once been you.) Yet somehow for the period of your existence they will answer to a single overarching impulse: to keep you you.

The bad news is that atoms are fickle and their time of devotion is fleeting.... When that time of devotion passes, for reasons unknown your atoms will shut you down, silently disassemble, and go off to be other things. And that's it for you.[45]

The large difference between modern science and Sāmkhya is that science does not provide a reason as to why these universal properties form. Bill Bryson summarizes that existence somehow emerges with form and ends as form disassembles, while Sāmkhya holds that existence is an eternal property of *purusha*. Accordingly, existence is not dependent on form, but pre-exists form. There is a reason and purpose for the assembly of these universal elements. They serve to provide experience and emancipation. Patañjali explains, "The seen, which has three attributes of light, movement and stability, projects into the elements and the organs, and serves the purpose of experience and emancipation (for the embodied one called *purusha*)."

---

[45] *A Short History of Nearly Everything*, page 1&2. The editor revised commentary to include this discussion.

Literally *purusha* means the indweller of the city. *Puri* means city and refers to the body. *Purusha* was defined as an all-pervasive knower, a being-ness of existence and consciousness. Its intrinsic quality of dwelling within every individual being forms an individual sense of self or the embodied one, also called *purusha*. The individual sense of self is the presence of the all-pervasive knower being adopted by an individual medium called *mahat* or intellect in Sāmkhya or *chitta* in Yoga.

This individual medium is a projection of nature. Its intrinsic quality is to adopt the properties of what is near it. It has two primary purposes. First, by adopting the qualities of the all-pervasive knower it enables one to have a personal, immanent experience of *purusha*. Understanding how this knower manifests within the medium comes with practice. Accepting our individual existence as one with this all-pervasive knower is emancipation.

Secondly, this medium is the holder of all the impressions, *samskaras*, of experience gained during a long process of evolution of this medium. The accumulated impressions form tendencies of behavior called *vāsanās*. As this medium is illuminated by *purusha* and becomes enlivened, the medium begins to modify. First, the impressions become active forming our *buddhi* or intellect. Our ability to think and decide is based on the accumulation of knowledge. Secondly, the *vāsanās* project forth as *ahamkāra*, our egoistic self, a collection of skills, abilities and behavioral patterns.

In our human form, nature manifests as our physical, mental, and intellectual bodies. When *purusha* manifests in the intellect, then the ego, the mind and senses, and the subtle elements appear as the subtle body. These organs gather around the causal body. This process is similar to the growth of a tree. A tree lives in a seed in subtle form until it gets the opportunity to sprout, growing branches, leaves and fruit. In the same way, the intellect is inspired by the light of spirit, and the ego, mind, senses, and subtle elements sequentially appear. Accumulation makes this possible.

Our intellect is the abode of pure knowledge and the cause of our individual life. The state of our intellect is formed by the impressions of our prior actions in this life and in previous lives. The impressions determine each situation we are born into. The subtle body has gathered impressions through many lifetimes, and in each life we perform action. In non-human species, action arises from instinct and is not prompted by the desire inherent within the law of *karma*. In human life, we retain the

41

impressions of all our actions, even from our experiences in non-human species. As humans, our actions are driven by our intentions and desires.

The belief that the physical body, the covering of our subtle body, is our real self is the fundamental impression of our continuous births. How many times we have been human, we cannot know. But we can be aware that our countless actions have created countless effects. Each time our *karma* ripens, it gives its fruit in the form of birth and determines our species, span of life, and circumstances. The span of life and the range of experiences are different for each of us. But for all of us, our current individual form, our abilities, and our outlook are structured by our previous actions.

We are most familiar with our gross physical body. The gross body is formed separately. It develops from the interaction of two parents and is nourished by the gross elements. The gross body, as with all physical form, is finite. When a subtle body is related with a gross body, we call that event birth; and when the subtle body separates from the gross body, we call that event death. Birth and death are related with the migration of the subtle body, not with *purusha*.

~~~

18
chaturdaśa-vidhah bhūta-sargah
Fourteen states of manifestated beings

Bhūta is a being and *sargah* is manifestation. This *sūtra* explains the evolution of manifested beings. The purpose of evolution is to develop our discriminative knowledge, enabling us to realize the source of our existence. Each individual medium develops through countless lifetimes. According to Sāmkhya, we develop through five lower stages: vegetation, insect, reptile, bird, and mammal before the subtle body gains a human body. Each being moves through eight and a half million species prior to gaining a human body. And it is only in human form that we are blessed with all of the necessary means for gaining experience and emancipation. These means are the instruments of the intellect, ego, mind, the five cognitive senses, and the five active senses.

Prior to gaining a human body, we develop over time through a natural process. The subtle body enters into, resides in, and then departs from the forms of many species. When we have evolved to the point where we reside in a human body, we have the potential for realization. We must appreciate this opportunity and commit ourselves to steady effort.

States of Manifested Beings		
Sattoguna States	**Rajoguna State**	**Tamoguna State**
brahmā loka	Human Form	Other Mammals
prājapāti loka		
indra loka		Bird
deva loka		Reptile
pitri loka		Insect
gandharva loka		Vegetation
rāksasa loka		
paisācha loka		

In addition to the five stages lower than human life, there are eight higher states. The eight higher levels are the divine *lokas*, and they are projections of *sattoguna*. A *loka* is a perceptible world. The first manifestation of nature is cosmic intellect. When this cosmic medium becomes enlivened by supreme consciousness it is called *Brahmā*. The first *sattvic* or divine world is the *brahmā loka*. The second projection is cosmic ego, *prājapāti loka*, and the third is cosmic mind, *indra loka*. The *deva loka* of the cognitive senses follows. *Deva* means divine. The cognitive senses are divine because they enlighten material objects with consciousness. The next level is *pitri loka*, the place of desires, also called the place of the ancestors. Our desires determine the circumstances of our lifetimes. Next comes *gāndharva loka*, the world of sensual pleasures. *Gāndharve* is a name for the active senses. The two lowest *lokas*, where souls travel between lives, are called *rāksasa loka* and *paisācha loka*. *Rāksasas* are infatuated with power and use force to meet their needs, and *paisāchas* use trickery, deceit, and cleverness to attain their goals. Beneath the eight levels of the *sattvic*, divine world, there is one projection of *rajoguna*, human life. And below human life there are the five stages that project through *tamoguna*: mammal, bird, reptile, insect, and vegetation. All three *gunas* are present at every level, but one particular *guna* dominates.

The five lower states are hell and the eight higher states are heaven. Heaven indicates a subtle world, a place without gross form. In the five levels of hell, we are bound by time, place and circumstances and are unable to use our intellects to seek higher truth. In these lower forms, we evolve through a natural process and are not empowered to seek wisdom. Once we have a human life, we must use it well.

Our actions produce either uplifting or painful results. And the impact of our actions lasts for a finite period of time. Even the results of beneficent action end at some point. In the heavenly worlds we enjoy the effects of our positive actions, but when those results finish, we return into human form. Heaven and hell are temporary. The individual soul eventually reemerges from heaven or hell, returning to a human body when the results of *karma* end. We should not waste this opportunity, as the development of the intellect and progress toward realization is only possible while we are human.

Our future circumstances depend on our behavior, our behavior is driven by our thoughts, and our thoughts are a product of the impressions we carry in the intellect. What we hold to be true is the foundation of our actions and beliefs. We must work to expand our understanding of truth and seek real knowledge. Knowledge lifts us higher, while ignorance, desire and blind faith cause our downfall. If we develop wisdom while we can, we move toward freedom and happiness. But if we pursue animal gratification instead, we squander this opportunity and move toward hell.

Wisdom distinguishes us as humans. Animals eat, sleep, and propagate their species. These behaviors are similar to human behavior. But if we humans behave only in these ways, we are no different from other animals. According to many scriptures, humans have the greatest potential in this world. We can uplift ourselves, experience oneness with our source, and perform divine service to all beings. We can seek illumination and knowledge, and realize truth.

The strength of a bulb depends on its wattage: the higher the wattage, the stronger the light. In the same way, the brilliance of consciousness adopted by a medium is determined by the capability of the medium to adopt consciousness. Our capacity is determined by our development as we evolve through many life forms. If *tamoguna* is dominant, the subtle body resides as a tree or a plant. With increasing amounts of *rajoguna*, we reside as an insect, reptile, bird or mammal. Once *rajoguna* becomes dominant and *sattoguna* increases sufficiently, the subtle body becomes the seed of a human. We humans are primarily *rajoguna*, but our abilities, knowledge and discrimination are enhanced by the influence of *sattoguna*.

Our circumstances arise from our actions, which are driven by our intentions. Until we refine our intellect, *rajasic* desire, in the form of lust, jealousy, anger, temptation, or greed, perpetuates our misery. As long as we believe this individual form is the self, our desires are selfish. If we only seek pleasures, we misuse our lives and accumulate *karma*, creating cycle after cycle of birth, misery and death. If we seek the truth, desiring to purify our intellect, we use our lives and resources for upliftment, and we gradually free ourselves. In human life alone, the laws of *karma* operate because we have the free will to choose our behaviors. Human life alone holds the potential for freedom. We must not waste this precious opportunity.

~~~

19
tri-vidhah bandhah
Three-fold bondage: causal, subtle, gross

Bondage and emancipation are related with the intellect. When the intellect is made pure, *purusha's* true form is known. The eight root causes (*prakritis*) and the sixteen modifications (*vikāras*) are the means for gaining knowledge and the objects of knowledge. These are the tools for having experiences and achieving emancipation.

Nature manifests by gathering these causes and modifications into our causal, subtle and gross bodies. Kapila has explained that *purusha* appears limited by manifesting in individual media. Now he teaches that when we accept a body as its form, we experience bondage.

A primary quality of manifest nature is finiteness, a limitation that may be thought of as a boundary. When we accept the limiting quality of nature and define our existence by this, we feel bound. There are three categories of bondage. First, *prākritika*, natural bondage, is related with the eight root causes of nature, which are the causal forms of nature. *Prakriti* is mistaken for the highest reality of *purusha*. Next is *dākshinika*, subtle bondage, related with our speculation about the nature of life and how to fulfill its purpose. When we are caught in this kind of bondage, we move through life with our focus on specific results or fruits of action. Our actions are influenced by our desire for personal gain. *Vaikārikā* is the gross level of bondage. It is the bondage of the senses, and is related with the *vikāras* or sixteen modifications. These are the eleven senses and the forms produced by the five primordial elements. At this level of bondage, we live to gratify the senses. We mistakenly worship the senses and the objects projected from nature.

We have three bodies: causal, subtle, and gross. The causal body is the medium that adopts the properties of *purusha*, an unbound consciousness of intelligence and existence. When our intellect adopts these qualities, it awakens with sentience and discernment. If we carry darkness and delusion, our intellect is dominated by *tamoguna*, and our capacity to discriminate is diminished. In this state, we cannot discriminate spirit from nature. This is *avidyā*, ignorance. Because we lack discernment, we think, "I am intelligent, I exist." We attribute the qualities of intelligence and existence to the limited individual medium, and we feel limited and separate.

This is *prākritika*, natural bondage. When our soul adopts the properties of the individual medium as its form, then infatuation, *moha*, develops as egoism. Feeling individual, limited and separate, we experience doubt and neediness. These feelings give rise to a greater infatuation, attachment. *Mahāmoha*, the great infatuation, turns the ego outwards. Experience gained outside the self becomes the source of our identity. We identify our sense of self with pleasures, status and relationships. We inevitably experience pain, giving rise to aversion, *tāmisra*.

We are bound in a world of comparisons and desires. Likes and dislikes are a dominant part of our experience. We experience the pleasures of attachment and develop passion. With passion come hate, greed and jealousy. Anger arises as we try to protect what we like and reject what we dislike. Attraction and aversion are natural responses to our identification with sensual experience.

With *vaikārika* bondage our identity is tied to experiences of the eleven senses and their related objects. If we are caught in this bondage, we are busy with worldly affairs, and our minds are infatuated with the stimulation of the senses. We may believe that this is the road to lasting satisfaction, but it leads to perpetual discontent. In the *Bhagavad Gīta*, Krishna tells us that, "The forces of the turbulent senses carry away the mind."[46] And later he builds on this idea: "Desire and wrath are begotten by *rajoguna*, insatiable and greatly injurious; know this to be the enemy;"[47]

---

[46] *Bhagavad Gīta* II.60.
[47] *Bhagavad Gīta* III.37.

When we are attached to any sense and its corresponding objects, sensual gratification dominates our state of mind. We constantly think about attaining and experiencing objects and relationships. This leads to a feeling of lack, as we constantly seek the next experience. In this state, we are always comparing ourselves to others, feeling superior if we have more and feeling jealous if we have less. When our desires are satisfied, we feel a moment of pleasure, which fuels our cravings and desperation for more experience. This binds us to the cycle of birth, misery, and death, and in each life we fall into worsening circumstances, including the possibility of life in a lower species. This is *vaikārikā* bondage. Our soul is bound in this cycle until we realize our real position of oneness with *purusha*. Wisdom leads us away from the natural attraction of physical attachment, the attachment of our soul with the projections of nature. In ignorance, we identify with the physical world, believing we are the body, senses, mind, and ego. We think in terms of "I" and "mine." Our possessive tendency can only be annihilated with pure knowledge, wisdom and understanding.

It is natural to accept the physical body as the self, but we are constantly reminded of our own mortality. We see many forms come into existence, age and die. The *Sāmkhya Kārikā* teaches that old age and death are the most painful experiences for the indweller.[48] The ultimate result of false knowledge is our great fear of death, *abhiniveśa,* also called blind aversion, *andha-tāmisra.* This is the fear of not having enough or of losing what we have. Mortality is our strongest fear and greatest enemy. We fear death because we do not understand it. Death is not related with *purusha.* It is related with the body. Our fear arises from our identification of the self with the gross body.

Humankind always seeks to alleviate the fear that comes from living in a gross body. We want salvation from death, an extension beyond physical life into eternal life. Religious practices, ritual sacrifices, services and donations are established to attain salvation in heaven. These activities are *dakshinika,* subtle bondage. Any ideas that heaven is permanent are mistaken. And actions undertaken for personal gain create limited *karmic* benefits. In heaven, souls receive the benefit of their previous virtuous actions. But the results of those actions wane over time, and then the soul and subtle body are reborn anew in human form.[49] Sāmkhya teaches that

---

[48] *Sāmkhya Kārikā* LV.
[49] *Yoga Sūtras* II-14.

we must have clear discrimination between nature and spirit to free ourselves from suffering.[50] If we analyze carefully, we find that all suffering comes from our ignorance. Kapila indicates that distinct awareness protects us from false knowledge. We want to be happy. The way to gain lasting happiness is to remove *tamoguna*, and then egoism. Remove passion and its companions of jealousy and hatred. Then the fear of loss and death are lifted. If we are ignorant of our true nature, we fear death. Ignorance is the cause of bondage and suffering.

~~~

20
tri-vidhah mokshah
Three-fold emancipation: gradual, disembodied, singleness

Emancipation, *mokshah*, is discussed in three ways and is dependent on an individual's prior evolutionary development. *Krama mukti* is gradual release. The *Bhagavad Gītā* describes this gradual process as: "Not only in one birth, but after many births, when a seeker performs higher practices, the seeker achieves emancipation."[51] It takes more than one life to become free. It takes time to reach emancipation. We can start our journey in any circumstances and with any state of mind. If we are dedicated, we will gradually ascend. Through many lifetimes, we climb toward emancipation, eventually freeing ourselves from the cycle of birth and death. This is *krama mukti*, gradual release.

Videha mukti is disembodied release. This relates to individual souls who are disembodied and live in higher *lokas*. Even though they have realized truth, they retain their individuality. Patañjali describes these souls as *videha-prakriti-layanah*. The word *videha* refers to a *yogi* who has achieved *ānanda samādhi*. *Prakriti laya* refers to a *yogi* who has achieved *asmitā samādhi*. When these types of *yogis* leave their bodies or become discarnate, they achieve a high place within the divine realm and live as emancipated souls. Whenever they take birth their realization returns without effort. They attain perfect emancipation when the dissolution of this cycle of evolution occurs.[52]

In *svarūpa-pratistha*, also called *kaivalya*, singleness, identity and experience of self is one with pure consciousness. In Yoga philosophy, this

---

[50] *Samkhya Kārikā* I and II.
[51] *Bhagavad Gītā* VII.19.
[52] *Yoga Sūtras* I-19.

is described as abiding in our own essence.[53] These *yogis* may choose to live in a physical body or a subtle body, but they live completely free within the full realization of truth. With doubtless knowledge, lustless love, and desireless service, they help others to free themselves.

~~~

21
tri-vidham pramānam
Three proofs: seeing, inference, testimony

There are three proofs for validating truth. *Pratyāksha, anumāna,* and *āgamah* are the means of evaluation.[54] *Yaksha* is to see, and *pratyāksha* means to see and realize truth directly. *Anumāna* is inferential truth; with wisdom we can infer truth. *Agamāh* is the testimony of souls who have realized truth.

Pratyāksha is commonly defined as visible evidence, but in all philosophical treatises, we learn that we do not see truth with our eyes. Truth is apprehended with internal awareness. The nose smells, the tongue tastes, the eyes see, the skin feels and the ears hear. Our five cognitive senses provide information about worldly objects. This information is processed by the mind, ego and intellect. The cognitive senses pass information to the mind and the mind presents information to the intellect. The intellect discriminates and determines what is to be accepted or rejected. If the intellect is not working well, then the mind will misguide us; causing us to collect and keep what ought to be rejected, and to dismiss what we should hold near. Without the light of intellect, we work against ourselves. We must refine our intellect to see the truth. *Pratyāksha* is the truth that can be seen and known by the intellect.

Inference, *anumāna,* is of three kinds: *pūrvavat, śesavat* and *sāmānyatodrsta.* *Pūrvavat* is when we infer an effect from a cause. For example, when we see a dark cloud we can infer rain is likely. *Śesavat* is when we infer the cause from an effect. If we sample a small amount of salty water from the sea, we can infer that seawater is salty. *Sāmānyatodrsta* is when we take information from one place and apply it to another location. For example, we observe that an apple tree is blooming in our yard, and we infer that apple trees are blooming across town.

---

[53] *Yoga Sūtras* IV-34.
[54] *Yoga Sūtras* I-7.

Testimony, *āgamāh*, is knowledge obtained from reliable sources including scriptures. In spiritual matters the teachings of *yogis* and *rishis* are often relied upon. Testimony can empower us to move toward truth. Sāmkhya philosophers believe that truth can be known. Each one of us is able to seek and realize ultimate truth.

~~~

22

etat samyak jnātvā kritkrityah syāt
na punastrividhena dhuhkhenānubhuyate
People who come to realize this knowledge will be free
from the effects of all actions and bondage, and will
never again be prey to threefold suffering.

When we attain perfect discrimination and realize truth, we experience emancipation. The actions of a realized, liberated person do not cause bondage. Like the wheel of a potter that keeps revolving after the pot is complete, a realized person remains active in life free from bondage.

The purpose of Sāmkhya philosophy is to free people from threefold suffering. The cause of threefold suffering is ignorance. Our ignorance exists as long as *rajoguna* or *tamoguna* dominate the intellect. When we have clear, complete *sattvic* knowledge of nature's transformations and spirit's inspiration, then we are free from threefold suffering.

The principal teaching is *heya, heya hetu, hāna, hānopāya. Heya* indicates future pain is to be avoided.[55] *Heya hetu* describes there is a cause of suffering, which is identification of the seer with the seen.[56] *Hāna* means that suffering can be removed.[57] And *hānopāya* proclaims there is a method to end suffering.[58] Suffering can be removed because pain is not a property of *purusha*, nor is it a property of nature. Pain comes from our infatuation—an extraneous experience that can be removed.

Patañjali instructs us to avoid the suffering that has not yet come. Past experiences of pain are over. Our current situation may be painful, but we cannot change the moment we have arrived in. What we can change is where we go from here. There is only one way to be free. We must adopt a process for seeking knowledge, thinking carefully, and realizing truth. We

---

[55] *Yoga Sūtras* II-16.
[56] *Yoga Sūtras* II-17.
[57] *Yoga Sūtras* II-25.
[58] *Yoga Sūtras* II-26.

have to use our own capacity and work with our own situation to free ourselves from bondage.

The *Yoga Sūtras*, which follow in the next section, offer guidance and practical methods for realizing truth.

Asato ma sad gamayā

Tamaso ma jyotīr gamayā

Mrityor ma amritam gamayā

Om Shantīh

May we be led from unreal to real

From darkness to light

From death to immortality

Om Peace

Yoga Sūtras

Section I—*Samādhi Pada*

Stable Intellect

I-1

atha yogānuśāsanam

Now, the teaching of Yoga.

Anuśasānam means discourse, indicating that Patañjali understands and follows the philosophy of Yoga, but he is not the originator of this philosophy. He compiled, and now explains the teachings of Yoga.

There is a story in the life of Buddha. Someone came to him and said, "Sir, I want to be a monk and a renunciant but I have some doubt. If you can remove my doubt then I will be your follower."

Buddha responded, "What is your doubt?"

The man said, "I have four troubling questions: When was this world created? Who created it? When did pain first come into the world? When did I first fall in this world and begin to suffer?"

Buddha answered him with a story. "My dear, once there was a person who liked to drink. One day he was intoxicated and he did not see the ditch next to him filled with sewage. He fell into the ditch. When he fell into that horror, his intoxication lifted and he cried out, 'Someone please rescue me from this place.'

"A person heard his crying, came to the ditch and said, 'My dear, catch my hand and I will pull you out.'

"The man replied, 'First answer my questions, then I will catch your hand and you can pull me out.'

"'What are your questions?'

"'When was this ditch dug? Who dug this ditch? When did filth come into this ditch? And when did I fall into this mess? Please tell me the answers to these questions, and then I can accept your help.'

"The man answered, "Oh my dear, when the ditch was dug who can say? I was not here. Who created it, I don't know. I don't know when it was polluted and I don't know when you fell into it, because I was not with you. But I know that this is an unhealthy place and if you stay here you will suffer. I can take your hand and bring you out. When you are out then you can get cleaned up and search for your own answers. If you are ready to come out I can help you. If you need answers first, then you are stuck there."

Buddha ended by saying, "I don't know when this world was created or who created it. When pain came in this world, I don't know. And I don't know when you fell in this world. I do know you are suffering, living a painful life. I can catch your hand, I can bring you out, and I can show you how to be free from pain. After you are free you can search for answers."

Sāmkhya and Yoga philosophers declare that this world exists as part of a natural, eternal process of evolution and involution. There is no finite creator, nor is there a beginning or ending. Suffering exists, and it is caused by ignorance of our own real nature. Our ignorance is the cause of our attachment to worldly things. Attachment leads to desire, and desire results in suffering. To be free from suffering, we must remove our ignorance.

We can find our footing in a dense darkness with only a small flashlight. Though a flashlight gives off a limited amount of light, it can show us the way one step at a time. If we wait for the whole path to be illuminated, we will never start our journey. Each of us has what we need to remove our ignorance. Yoga gives us methods for using our own limited human capacities to find eternal freedom from suffering.

We must see where we need to make progress on our spiritual path. First we accept the conditions of our life and acknowledge our own abilities. With a realistic evaluation we begin one step at a time. An ideal guides us, but we implement changes gradually. We can appreciate our healthy, helpful behaviors and see where we need to make changes. Now is always the time to dedicate ourselves to our efforts.

~~~

I-2
yogaś citta-vrtti-nirodhah
Yoga is stilling the modifications of *chitta*.

In *sūtras* I-2 through I-4, Patañjali explains the gist of Yoga. Yoga is stilling the modifications of *chitta*.[59] *Chitta* is a subtle receptor at the top of our head, which is the medium for receiving, holding and reflecting consciousness. The special property of *chitta* is its ability to adopt and receive what is near to it. It reflects the qualities of what is close by and

---

[59] There is no equivalent word for *chitta* in English. Attempts to translate *chitta* are often misleading and fail to develop a proper understanding this concept.

holds that reflection so the qualities can be experienced. It can be simply described as a medium. In *sutra* I-41, Patañjali compares *chitta* to a crystal jewel. If red flowers are next to a clear crystal, it will appear to be red. The crystal is pure, but it adopts redness from the nearby flowers. The most important ability of the limited medium of *chitta* is to adopt the qualities of spirit, bringing into our lives a lively intelligence, a stable existence and an unwavering feeling of bliss. These three together are called consciousness.

Chitta is the primary causal form of nature and it is an individual medium. It manifests the qualities of all-pervading spirit, and adds its particular shape of individuality to spirit. Understanding that there are two distinct properties blended when spirit enlivens the *chitta* is fundamental to understanding Yoga. The Vedas highlight this blending with the example of an iron ball. When an iron ball is placed in fire, the ball looks like a red mass of fire. Because an iron ball has the potential to receive the element of fire, it appears to be a ball of fire.[60] When fire, which has no distinct shape, joins with the iron ball, it assumes the form of a red ball. In reality, there are two distinct entities—fire and iron.

In the same way, *chitta*, which is a medium of nature, has the potential to adopt and receive the qualities of spirit, pure consciousness. Like fire lighting the iron ball, spirit brings the quality of sentience to insentient nature. And as the iron ball gives shape to fire, the *chitta* gives individual form to the presence of consciousness. Thus, we experience consciousness as individual and personal when this unbound intelligence and existence is adopted by the individual medium.

The word *chitta* comes from the Sanskrit root *chit*, which means intelligence. Our individual *chitta* is the receptor of consciousness in our body. It is a tiny space just below the *brahma chakra* at the top of the head. It is the place where pure consciousness manifests in the human body. Because *chitta* is a projection of nature, it is inanimate, insentient, and changeable. When enlivened by pure consciousness it becomes as if animate, sentient and intelligent.

The light of pure consciousness is necessary for *chitta* to become enlivened. Just as light is necessary for a crystal to be revealed as pure or to receive colors from other objects, consciousness is required for *chitta* to become active. Sāmkhya tells us that when spirit manifests in nature, it

---

[60] *Rig* and *Yajur Vedas.*

inspires movement. [61] This movement causes nature to project, transforming pure nature into all things. The many variations of the projection of nature are referred to as modifications or effects. [62] *Chitta* transforms when it adopts consciousness. The *chitta* produces the intellect, ego, and mind. The intellect is our power to discriminate, the ego is the doer, the actor, and the mind translates our experience into what can be known.

These three modifications—intellect, ego and mind—are the modifications of *chitta* which are to be stilled. When this is attained, a state of Yoga, the unity of individual consciousness with pure consciousness, can be experienced and realized. This is the experience described in the next *sutra:* the seer is established in its own qualities.

Yoga offers methods for developing discernment, the capacity to discern the seer from the seen. Discernment frees the seer from identifying with the seen, which endlessly fluctuates, inflates our self-importance, and triggers our attachments. When we do not realize that consciousness manifests within us as our self, we attribute the limiting effects of the natural world to our own self. We imagine that our existence is limited and finite. This ignorance is defined in *sutra* II-3 as wrong thinking, and it pollutes our ability to see clearly.

We begin to still the modes of *chitta* and learn to see clearly by working to control our emotions. Emotions are stirred up by the speculation that takes place in the mind. Emotions trigger desire, and desire becomes a source of frustration, restlessness, desperation and dejection in our minds. Uncontrolled emotions cause us suffering. We know we suffer. We know the pain of our suffering. In spite of that, suffering is common and the search for lasting happiness is rare.

Yoga offers practices for transforming our emotions into devotion, bringing tranquility into our lives. Consciousness is eternal and unchangeable; all other things in life change in every moment. Change is intrinsic to nature. It cannot be stopped, nor can worldly desire be fulfilled. When we channel our emotional energy into devotion, our emotional dramas transform into devotional happiness.

Most of us make enormous efforts to achieve worldly goals. If half of our efforts would be directed toward the source of our self we would find

---

[61] See *Tattva Samāsa* 5.
[62] See *Tattva Samāsa* 2 and 3.

what we are truly seeking. Unfortunately, few of us are eager to begin the search for something intangible. We can easily see the things around us, but we rarely try to see what is within us. Divinity is within us, abiding in our *chitta*. When we stop the senses from seeking pleasure and seek inward to fulfill our inner demand for wholeness, then divinity can be experienced.

~~~

I-3
tadā drastuh svarūpe 'vasthānam
Then the seer abides in itself.

Patañjali uses seer for pure consciousness, so the seer is one infinite and all-pervasive consciousness. The seer is present in every medium nature projects. It is indivisible, unlimited and does not become divided or limited when indwelling the projections of nature. This presence of consciousness is similar to space. Space is all-pervading and exists both in and out of all containers. It seems as if space is defined by specific containers, but the containers merely define a boundary of space.

Therefore, when nature projects into form this medium, *chitta*, having the ability to adopt that which is near it, adopts the qualities of consciousness and the individual medium becomes as if conscious and existent. This first stage of the enlivened medium is explained as consciousness dwelling within a body. The Sanskrit term for this experience of dwelling within is *purusha*—"that which dwells within a city." Here the boundary of the city is the causal body, *chitta*. The indweller is a combination of the individual medium, "I," and the quality of conscious existence.

The experience of *purusha* is "I exist" or "I-am." In other systems of thought this stage is called *jīvātmā*, individual soul. The all-pervasive presence of pure consciousness becomes defined by the individual medium, as space is defined by its boundaries. Yet, the indweller or soul retains the qualities of consciousness. The *Sāmkhya Kārikā* explains that the indweller is endowed with the characteristics of witnessing, isolation, indifference, perception and inactivity.[63] Therefore, the indweller remains separate from the *chitta* as an unbound witness of its modifications.

---

[63] *Sāmkhya Kārikā* XIX.

The seer is pure consciousness. The properties of spirit remain unchanged when it indwells the medium of nature. The seer appears to dwell within, yet it is all-pervading and without limits. The limits and boundaries we experience are the limits of nature. The mind and intellect along with the senses present information to this indweller for its experience and emancipation. We attribute all-pervading consciousness to our individual consciousness. In reality our individual consciousness is part and parcel of an all-pervading seer or knower. As we define space by the boundaries we create, we define our existence by the boundaries of *chitta*, superimposing limits on our seer. Spirit does not just reside in nature, but pervades nature.

Spirit is one and absolute. The media of manifestation are countless. Each medium defines the limits of the container in which all-pervasive consciousness resides. When spirit dwells within the many *chittas* of our human forms, it is called individual *purusha* or individual soul. The same qualities of spirit—intelligence, existence, and bliss—reside within every medium. And when the seer is experienced within the medium, unattached to the modifications of *chitta*, the seer realizes its own state of pure consciousness. Yoga establishes this truth. Emancipation from suffering comes as we establish our identity within the seer, within pure consciousness.

~~~

I-4
vrtti-sārūpyam itaratra
Otherwise, the self is identified with the modifications of *chitta*.

Movement begins when consciousness manifests in the *chitta*. This movement awakens the medium and it becomes as if intelligent and existent. The light of pure consciousness is necessary for the *chitta* to be active, just as a power source is necessary for a light bulb to give light. The commingling of consciousness with *chitta* inspires the *chitta* to modify, initiating the self-awareness of I-amness. I-amness is a subtle experience. It is the indication that consciousness is present in the medium.

Chitta is a part of inanimate, insentient nature. Alone, *chitta* is like a vacant house, with no life or movement inside. As mentioned, its intrinsic quality is to adopt the properties of what is near it. It adopts in two ways. First, by adopting the qualities of the all-pervasive seer it enables one to have a personal, immanent experience of pure consciousness. Secondly, this medium is the holder of all the impressions, *samskaras*, of experience gained during a long process of evolution of the medium. The accumulated impressions structure our beliefs and form tendencies of behavior called *vasanas*. As *chitta* adopts consciousness it modifies in three ways.

The first modification is the intellect. As the impressions become active, we develop the ability to discriminate and make judgments. Secondly, the accumulated tendencies project forth as our ego self, which is a collection of skills, abilities and behavioral patterns. The ego is an active power. We can observe our ego at work through our attractions and aversions. The third modification of the medium is the mind. All the activity of the intellect and ego appear in the mind as thinking, deciding, sentiments, and emotions. These appear as waves of thought called *manas*.

We become identified with these three modifications of *chitta*, the intellect, ego and mind. We mistakenly think that we are this capacity to discriminate and discern, but it is actually just the function of the intellect. Also, our experience of existence is mistakenly associated with the ego. And we become attached to the imaginative thoughts, speculations, and range of experiences which appear in the mind.

When consciousness manifests in nature, nature projects the means for us to experience consciousness. Understanding how consciousness manifests within the medium comes with knowledge and experience. Accepting our individual existence as one with this all-pervasive consciousness is emancipation. When we define our sense of self by the constraints of the tools we are given, we experience limitation, bondage and suffering. When we realize the truth of our existence and understand that these tools of nature are enlivened by consciousness, we are freed from our suffering.

People who rent houses come to think of them as home. This is only natural, but like these tenants, we forget that we are temporary occupants. We forget that our *chitta*, along with every aspect of our physical existence, is only a projection of nature. It is part of nature and belongs to nature. Because we identify with these limited forms we accept this limited, individual existence as our own self. The continued acceptance of this wrong thinking develops into impressions or modes of thinking that reside within our *chitta* and form our intelligence. We come to believe we are separate from consciousness, the source of our self. Because we identify with limitation, we feel deficient and empty, and attempt to fulfill ourselves by accumulating more and more objects of nature. We seek outside of the self. We are seeking happiness by chasing endless accumulation. This only stimulates further desire. All of this movement is reflected in our *chitta* through the mode of the mind. This activity disturbs our ability to see and discriminate clearly.

The intellect discriminates between truth and fiction. The ego accepts or rejects experiences, and the mind reflects what is experienced, stirring up our infatuations and our fears. When we become identified with the push and pull of the mind, we suffer. Great suffering is caused by our desire to own and to control. Our self-imposed feelings of misery and imprisonment are triggered by our obsessions with people, things and situations. When we draw the mind inward and turn toward the infinite source of all things, we experience happiness and emancipation.

The mind is not unique in its capacity to keep us in confusion and suffering. If the ego accepts the body as its own existence, then we live in fear of death. Just as the mind can turn toward its source in consciousness, the ego can turn, accept I-amness as the presence of consciousness, and experience eternal existence. As the mind relinquishes desire and becomes quiet, the ego can turn and surrender toward the source.

The intellect is closest to our source of life. At the level of the intellect, our lack of discrimination causes us to feel adrift and isolated in a sea of diversity. When we face outward, we live through our senses and identify with sensation and sensational dramas. It is our fundamental ignorance in the intellect that causes the ego and mind to face outward. Our identification with and attachment to the body, the senses, and the objects of the senses creates confusion and anxiety at all levels of our being. We must work our way back in, quieting the mind, aligning the ego and seeking truth in the intellect.

~~~

I-5
vrttayah pañcatayyah klistāklistāh
The modifications are either painful or not painful and appear in five varieties.

The fluctuations of these modifications are as innumerable as waves on the ocean. They may be painful, *klishtā*, or painless, *aklishtā*, and a modification that is painful for one person may not be painful for another.

It is easy to see how our fears bring us pain, but we may be unaware that our desires also cause our suffering.

This *sutra* explains that the opposite of pain is not pleasure, but neutrality. *Aklishta* is a neutral state that does not lead to the pain that arises from either adversity or pleasure. Patañjali clearly states that we cannot find lasting peace or happiness through identification with any modification of *chitta*. Our thoughts and impulses related with worldly things are either fearful or lustful, and both fear and desire are insatiable. Anxieties and passions feed on themselves and grow ever larger. When we seek security or happiness through worldly things, we will never be at peace and we will never find lasting happiness. Everything in the natural world is always in a state of flux, and it is impossible to find lasting safety or satisfaction in a constantly changing world.

We cannot protect ourselves from painful experiences and it is fruitless to seek only pleasant experiences. This is central to Yoga philosophy: all fluctuations of the *chitta* are to be stilled. Pain is caused by our attachment, whether we are attached to our aversions, our pleasures, or both. Seeking enjoyment through worldly objects in the hope that one day we will achieve lasting happiness is pointless. All of nature is transitory, including our faculties. When we lose our faculties of perception, when we lose our ability to gain experience and information from the world around us, we suffer. Patañjali declares that if we want to be free from suffering, then we must make an effort to still the modifications of *chitta* and thereby realize our own true nature in pure consciousness. In this way we become free from suffering. There is no other way.

When a person quiets the modifications of the intellect, ego and mind, the *chitta* clears and the real form of the self can be realized as it appears in *chitta*. In stillness, the *chitta* remains receptive and the mode of intellect is directed toward divinity. This state is called *brahmvritti*, which means the *vrittis* have turned from worldly affairs and become aligned with the supreme cause. Krishna avows: "This is the divine state. Having attained this, the practitioner is not deluded and is fixed in the self."[64] This is the purpose of Yoga. This highest good is unwavering and it is the only path to lasting fulfillment.

~~~

---

[64] *Bhagavad Gītā* II.72.

I-6
pramāna-viparyaya-vikalpa-nidrā-smrtayah
The five varieties are correct evaluation, misconception, speculation, deep sleep, and memory.

These five appear in the intellect, ego and mind as *pramāna*, correct evaluation; *viparyaya*, misconception; *vikalpa*, speculation; *nidrā*, deep sleep; and *smriti*, memory. Each one of these is explained in the next five *sutras*.[65]

~~~

I-7
pratyaksānumānāgamāh pramānāni
Pramāna, correct evaluation, is of three types: perception, inference and valid testimony.

The Sanskrit root of *pramāna* means to measure perfectly. *Pramāna* is correct assessment. Our intellect measures through perception, inference, and valid testimony. Perception, *pratyaksha*, is seeing directly through one of our senses. Inference, *anumāna*, uses our logic based on previous proofs. Valid testimony, *āgamāh*, is authoritive knowledge of a reliable person. Right knowledge is dependent upon a clear, unbiased evaluation of experience. We measure everything in this world with our intellects. This is true whether we are measuring something tangible and visible or something subtler that can only be felt or perceived. As the intellect assesses everything we see and experience, we gain knowledge.

Pratyāksha literally means "in front of the eyes." Here, *aksha*, eyes, refers to our capacity to see using all of our active and cognitive senses.[66] All of our senses gather information and offer a unique way to see the world. Among our five cognitive senses, the tongue perceives by taste, skin by touch, nose by smell, ears by sound, and eyes by form. Our active senses also provide information. For example, we can estimate weight by holding an object in our hands. All our cognitive and active senses help us to measure and to see. The cognitive senses are an extension of the intellect, and the active senses are the instruments of the intellect. Our ten

---

[65] See also *Tattva Samāsa* 9.

[66] The ten senses, the *indriyas*, are the five cognitive senses of taste, smell, form, touch, and hearing, and the five active senses of walking, grasping, speaking, eliminating, and procreating. Of the five organs of action—the legs, hands, tongue, eliminative and sexual organs—the tongue is unique in that is relates with two functions: taste and speech.

senses provide information to the intellect and the intellect works through the senses.

Inference is the ability to draw a conclusion about one thing from the knowledge we have of another. Inference is related with cause and effect and is based on recognized knowledge or seen knowledge. Scientific analysis and its working theories are based on this type of logic. There are three kinds of inference related with the past, present and future. For example, relying on the past knowledge of weather conditions, we can infer that rain is coming when seeing dark clouds and feeling moisture in the air. An example in the present is that of a researcher analyzing a sample to infer knowledge about a larger quantity. If a sample of ocean water is salty, the rest of the ocean is salty. Lastly, when observing a bud developing into a blossom, we can infer that fruit and leaves will develop in the near future and that spring is following winter.

Valid testimony is dependent upon the reliability and the motive of the person providing the knowledge. In spiritual matters, we rely upon the testimony of *yogis* and *rishis*, those who have realized truth. This testimony is found in scriptures or gained by listening to a teacher. The testimony of a realized person may guide us, but we must purify and stabilize our own intellect to fully understand the teachings. This teaching is not about blind faith, but about reasoning, questing and realizing. We must apply that knowledge in our own lives.

We strive to understand whatever is within our own reach or vision. We cannot afford to be lazy or to accept blindly the word of another. The gross world is known through perception. Objects that cannot be directly perceived by the senses can be proved through inference. The imperceptible can be understood through valid testimony. Whatever is beyond the gross and subtle can be relied upon using testimony, until one day, upon reaching the highest state; we can personally realize truth.

~~~

I-8
viparyayo mithyājñānam atad-rūpa-pratistham
Reverse knowledge is misconception regarding worldly things.

Pramāna is related with proof; it is the intellect seeking truth; it favors reasoning and logic; it values discernment; and it acts with correct evaluation. *Viparyaya* is the opposite: it believes without proof, reacts without logic or discernment, seeks false security and momentary pleasures, and incorrectly assesses the circumstances of life. *Viparyaya* always leads to suffering.

Our ignorance is any incorrect evaluation of life. In the second chapter Patañjali states: "Ignorance is accepting the finite, impure, suffering-inducing, non-self as the eternal, pure, blissful real self."[67] When our I-amness manifests in a body with senses, it easily believes that the body and senses are where life begins and ends. This is ignorance. *Viparyaya* means that our thinking flows counter to the current of truth. Our reverse knowledge relies on what seems true but is, in fact, wrong. If we readily accept what seems true rather than searching for truth, we become the easy prey of infatuation. We become attached to our bodies and our sensual experiences, which fills us with fear and desire.

Patañjali further elaborates how wrong knowledge leads to a state of suffering in *sūtras* II-3 through 9. He states that ignorance is the root cause of our suffering, and is followed by egoism, attachment, aversion, and finally a state of fear and anxiety. Through this counter current of reverse knowledge, we move away from the truth that is our source of lasting peace and happiness.

~~~

I-9
sabda-jñānānupātī vastu-śūnyo vikalpah
Speculation is using words that have meaning but no substance.

Vikalpa, fanciful thinking, fuels our belief in things that do not exist. The inverse also applies in *vikalpa*: in this kind of thinking we fail to believe in the truth. Once we supplant reality with our imaginative thinking, we feed our speculation in every possible way. It is said that if we repeat a lie one hundred times then it is accepted as truth. When we hear something often enough it becomes an accepted truth, even if it has no basis in reality. This is *vikalpa*, and, sadly, we spend our precious energy fueling our assumptions. It has never been possible to fulfill our desire in the material world, yet we are bombarded with messages that tell us we can, and we continue to try. This is a powerful example of fanciful thinking.

The speculation of *vikalpa* happens constantly. Our belief that we can search for happiness in the world of things is based on what we have heard and on our own fantasies. We chase after whatever we desire, and

---

[67] *Yoga Sūutras* II-5.

yet when we have attained our goals, we find that the pleasure of achievement is fleeting. We soon begin to fantasize about a new goal. We will never find lasting happiness until we realize that truth and bliss reside inside, not outside.

The sage Vyasa notes that people consider knowledge to be a quality of the soul that can exist separate from the soul, but the soul itself is knowledge and consciousness. If we say that salt is salty, it implies that saltiness exists separate from salt, but this is not possible. Salt exists in saltiness and saltiness exists in salt. Intelligence, existence and bliss are the qualities of the true self; these three qualities are the soul and the soul is these three qualities. Our thinking that worldly things can offer us these qualities and provide happiness is *vikalpa*; our ideas lack substance. We can only find lasting happiness within the true self.

~~~

I-10
abhāva-pratyayālambanā vrttir nidrā.
The absence of experience in the intellect is called deep sleep.

Pratyaya means experience, and *abhāva* means lack or absence. In the waking state the intellect is involved with experiences. In the dreaming state the intellect remembers experience. *Nidrā* is the deep sleep state when the intellect is without experience and it rests in its source in causal nature. In the transition toward sleep, *sattoguna* yields to *rajoguna* and we feel a lack of focus. As *rajoguna* gradually succumbs to *tamoguna*, we slumber. If a little *rajoguna* remains active, we dream. In the dream state, we are aware of ourselves as individuals because our egos are still working. Dreaming, we roam in a dream world of diversity, experiencing happiness, fear and pain. When dense *tamoguna* covers the intellect, we sleep deeply and do not dream. This deep sleep state brings peace and ecstasy that is different from the pleasure related to sensual and emotional thoughts and feelings. Ecstasy is an experience of the self and the source, without the limitations of individual experiences.

In deep sleep we have no knowledge of ourselves as individuals and no awareness of others. The universe exists, but we have no comprehension of it. In deep sleep, the mind merges into the ego, the senses are quiet and we lose awareness of the body. The ego is active in the waking state. In the state of deep sleep, we have no knowledge of the world and the ego merges into the intellect, which in turn rests quietly, and the *chitta* becomes still.

Thinking, working and engaging with the world exhaust us. We need sleep to restore ourselves. When the ego is active, we deplete our energy, and without sleep we cannot think clearly or function well. When exhaustion overcomes us, we know that we need to sleep deeply. In *nidrā* we re-energize. In this deep sleep state the ego is quiet. We rest in our source and receive energy from our source. And yet *nidrā* is a state of *tamoguna*, darkness and inertia, which is why moderation in sleep is advised. As in all practices of Yoga, we must seek balance.

One of the blessings of meditation is that it teaches us to reach into a state of deep rest while alert. *Samādhi* means a stable and even intellect. The intellect is fully awake but without an external focus. Similar to deep sleep, *samādhi* is a state where all diversity disappears.

~~~

I-11
anubhūta-visayāsampramosah smrtih
Memory is the recollection of a previous experience.

In the modification called memory, we recall the impressions stored from our direct experience, inference and studies. *Smriti* refers to the knowledge we firmly hold. This specific mental activity does not include new information being gained in the present moment. It is the reconstruction of the past that comes in the present. Our ability to store new memories is dependent on our previous skill in holding and recalling past events. Memory rooted in *sattoguna*, radiance and light, is developed with an even intellect.

With memory we can understand how a mode of thought is either painful or non-painful. Painful memories can cause distraction or depression. Our perception can be clouded by our memories. In meditation all kinds of repressed and forgotten memories may return.

~~~

I-12
abhyāsa-vairāgyābhyām tan-nirodhah
The modifications of *chitta* can be stilled by practice and detachment.

When we realize we have a habit or behavior that causes trouble in our lives, and we decide to make a change, we try to stop the old behavior and

66

implement a new behavior. Patañjali describes this process as practice and detachment. We detach or restrain from an old way of thinking and begin to establish a new way of thinking in order to experience the true qualities of self.

Yoga is establishing our identity in the qualities of the seer, an all-pervasive intelligence and existence. The practices of Yoga are specific tools for shifting our identity away from worldly objects and relationships. We alone create feelings of separation and lack. We alone can free ourselves by establishing our identity in the qualities of the seer, the one who knows and sees this ever-changing world. We are responsible for detaching from the modes or habits of thinking that prevent us from experiencing our real self. No one else can do this for us. We must establish our identity in the seer.

Practice and detachment are related with Sāmkhya. Sāmkhya suits the practitioner who is more intellectually inclined. On this path, logic and analysis are primary. The practice of meditation is the effort of searching for the self. It inherently requires turning away from the stimulation of the senses and the identification of the self with the modifications of the intellect, ego, and mind and the modes of thinking that limit our existence. Practice requires detachment. Sāmkhya provides the framework for understanding that the self is the seer, and that everything we detach from is the seen. Our lives are a projection of spirit and nature, and Sāmkhya indicates that we need to understand both in order to be established in the self.

Krishna gives the same teaching in the *Bhagavad Gītā*: "Without a doubt, O mighty one, the mind is difficult to restrain, but by practice and by indifference, it is restrained."[68] It is not possible to practice without detachment. If we are too attached with the modifications of *chitta*, we cannot make the effort required for practice. *Vairāgya* is sometimes called dispassion. The dispassion required for practice means we turn away from the stimulation of the outer world and its temptations. Then our practice can be successful. We must disentangle from our attachments and turn toward the seer.

We all wish for the eternal, divine bliss that we experienced when our individual *chitta* first adopted pure consciousness. The stirring of this initial contact naturally generates a constant quest to return to that feeling of

---

[68] *Bhagavad Gītā* VI.35.

bliss and discover its source. Our mental restlessness will never be removed until this desire is fulfilled. Because of our ignorance and illusion, the mind seeks to fulfill this inner demand for oneness through the effects of nature's projection rather than with the original source. The ego turns its face toward the world of the senses and their objects, and we engage in countless activities that cannot fulfill this demand for eternal, divine bliss. Because of our illusions, we feel separate and misdirect our search to fulfill our inner demand for blissful unification with the source.

It is ironic and tragic that we consider ourselves separate from our source. Practice helps us recognize this misunderstanding. Our inner demand is to be free from the suffering caused by separation from our source. Practice requires effort. We must turn away from our attempts to find oneness in the external world and realize it inside.

~~~

I-13
tatra sthitau yatno 'bhyāsah
The effort to create stability there (seer) is called practice.

Practice is the effort to establish the self in its own qualities. The word *tatra* means there. Patañjali uses this word to indicate the experience of the seer abiding in itself, pure consciousness.[69] In *sūtra* I-4, Patañjali says that without Yoga the seer identifies with the modifications of *chitta* and subsequent modes of thinking. Practice is needed to shift our identity and establish it within the seer.

Practice is the process of meditation. Knowledge we receive from teachers and scriptures makes us aware of the qualities of our true self, and meditation is the way to realize this knowledge for ourselves. We become aware that what we previously accepted as the self, such as the body, senses, ego and mind, is not our real self. Knowing this, we search beyond all forms and turn the modes of our thinking inward to search for the seer, which is above these forms.

The seer is pure consciousness. Nature, the seen, comes into form, sustains for a period of time, and then dissolves out of form. The self, adopting the medium of nature, becomes identified with this cycle and experiences a separate, finite, limited, and unstable existence within the human body. This experience of limitation and instability is suffering.

---

[69] "There" refers to *sūtra* I-3, "then the seer abides in itself."

According to the *Taittirīya Upanishad*, the soul functions through five levels called sheaths, *kośas*. These five sheaths cover this indweller. The *kośas* are *annāmāyā*, *prānamāyā*, *manomāyā*, *vijñānamāyā*, and *ānandamāyā*, which can be translated as body, senses, mind, intelligence, and bliss.[70] In our human life, these are described as levels of consciousness. When consciousness manifests in our *chitta* and appears as bliss consciousness, there is no individual or separate quality at this highest level. Consciousness is present in the form of intelligence, existence and bliss. These qualities are the appearance of our source residing with us as seer. When pure consciousness enlivens our *chitta*, the *chitta* modifies or projects as our discriminative function of the *vijñānamāyā kośa* called intelligence consciousness.

The form of our intellect appears as waves of thought called mind consciousness. Following mind consciousness, the final two coverings of the self are senses consciousness and body consciousness. These are called breath consciousness and food consciousness in the *Taittirīya Upanishad*. When our minds are focused on the external world, our experiences related with the objects of the senses and our emotional attachments related with our physical bodies clutter the mind and cover the pure perception of the self. In a pure intellect, the inner self is seen clearly as a reflection in a mirror. When the blending of self with form begins, the mind becomes more active and our inner perception becomes less clear—it is hazy or fragmented as a reflection in cloudy, rippling water. As the intellect turns inward, these disturbances settle, and the intellect clearly reflects the seer manifesting as our individual self.

The goal of spiritual practice is to realize the presence of the seer. The intellect discriminates between the seer and seen. Awareness develops in stages and is based on the understanding that all forms are projections of nature. The seer is entirely formless, beyond and above nature, yet pervading all. Through discrimination we realize that eternal happiness and bliss are properties of the seer.

Discrimination starts at the gross level of form and moves inward towards the self. In the *Taittirīya Upanishad* there is a story of Brighu, who approaches his father, Varuna, and requests to understand ultimate truth. His father tells him that *Brahman* is that from which this whole universe

---

[70] *Taittirīya Upanishad* II.2 through 7.

came, that by which this whole universe is sustained, and that in which this universe will merge. That is ultimate reality.

Brighu asks his father to give him a process by which he can realize and understand ultimate truth for himself. His father tells him that it requires austerity and discrimination: detachment and practice. With this, Brighu begins his inward search. He thinks deeply on the cause of life, how is it sustained, and where it goes when it is finished.

After some time he returns to his father and says he has realized ultimate truth is food.[71] "All beings come from food, once born all beings are sustained by food, and in the end all beings merge back into food. Therefore, food is *Brahman*."

His father says, "Okay, but examine more deeply now." He does not indicate that Brighu is wrong, nor criticize his understanding, but tells him to proceed further.

With this encouragement Brighu continues his practice by thinking more deeply. He realizes that *prāna* is required for obtaining and for digesting food. Breath is coming and going in this body and because of breath our senses are activated and digestive power works. Without breath we could not digest the food we take. He decides that breath is *Brahman* and goes to his father and master to explain this to him.

His father says, "Good, but proceed further."

Now, Brighu thinks more deeply. Breath is the cause of gastric fire. Breath activates this body and with breath we are able to acquire and digest food, which nourishes this body. Food is necessary for life. Breathing is important for digestion and activity, but the mind must decide whether to take food or not. My mind chooses what food to collect with my senses. So mind is the truth behind this world and must be the absolute truth.

Again he returns to his father to explain his realization. His father smiles, and encourages him to proceed.

Brighu begins to dwell on what could be the source of his mind. Gradually he realizes that his intelligence is at the root of his mind. If his intelligence and consciousness are not present, then his mind would not work and life would not exist for him. "My mind is a series of waves of thought made possible by my intelligence. So my intelligence and

---

[71] Food indicates matter.

awareness must be the source of my life. This individual intelligence and consciousness must be *Brahman*."

With great excitement, Brighu returns from his austere practices and tells his father that he has realized that intelligence is *Brahman*.

His father is pleased with Brighu's efforts and tells him that he is very near to ultimate truth and encourages him to proceed a little further.

Brighu searches more deeply for the cause of his own individual intelligence and consciousness. In the end he discovers bliss. Bliss is the cause of life, and all that is seen comes from bliss, is sustained by bliss, and merges back into bliss. "This bliss is my real self and is pure knowledge and consciousness. There is no separation in bliss. It is infinite and eternal. Bliss is *Brahman*." When he realizes this fact he does not return to his father for affirmation. He is fully satiated and experiences eternal peace and tranquility.

~~~

I-14
sa tu dīrgha-kāla-nairantarya-satkārāsevito drdha-bhūmih
Continuous practice with devotion for a long period of time gives firmness.

Practice and detachment require continuous, uninterrupted effort over a long time. We do not succeed by working one day and taking the next day off. Even after a few years, we should not take a break. Constant practice without interruption is needed.

We must have respect, *satkāra*, for our practice. If we are not devoted to practice, if we doubt our process and wonder whether we are on the right path, we cannot be steadfast. No progress comes in this way. Healthy inquiry deepens our practice, but doubt weakens practice.

By dedicating ourselves for a long time with respect towards our practice we develop a stable mind and a foundation in the seer.

~~~

I-15
drstānusravika-visaya-vitrsnasya vasīkāra-sañjñā vairāgyam
Detachment is when the seeker has no desire for worldly objects or experiences described by others.

There are two categories of objects that create temptation in our minds—gross and subtle. Gross refers to the visible realm, worldly objects of enjoyment that surround our everyday life. The subtle refers the perceptible, but intangible, such as ideas of heaven and subtle powers that draw us into attachments.

Vairāgya, detachment, is the absence of *rāga*, attachment. *Rāga* is the attraction or attachment to situations, people and objects that give us pleasure. Detachment occurs when we stop expecting happiness from people, places and things. *Vairāgya* is often confused with *tyāga*, renunciation, and it is important to understand the difference. Renunciation is physical isolation from the objects of temptation, whereas detachment is the cessation of the expectation that we will gain happiness from external attachments. A renunciant may be clinging to dreams of external fulfillment, in spite of an austere life. True detachment is experienced only when lived among the abundance of objects.

Rather than shutting out the world, Patañjali emphasizes observing experience in the light of knowledge. Our detachment is not affected by the presence or absence of objects unless we place value on the experience. Desire creates feelings of loss when our cravings are unfulfilled and joy when we are satiated. These emotions are related with our desires and not our needs. A need is a requirement of life and must be fulfilled. When we analyze worldly experiences and things, we can determine their value for us.

There is a story about a famous saint and singer in South India named Purandardas. He was poor, lived in a small hut, and begged for alms. When the king learned of him, he requested his prime minister to arrange a visit so he could listen to him sing. Upon arriving at the small hut, the king met the saint's wife and discovered that the saint was out begging. While waiting, the king questioned his prime minister as to how such a great saint and famous singer could live in such conditions.

When the saint joined them, the king requested that he sing. The saint took his instrument and began singing songs of the glory of God. The king was moved, and after the last song he said to the saint, "I am not pleased that a divine soul such as you is living within my kingdom in these conditions."

"It may not be acceptable to you," the saint replied, "but for me this is a divine place. You are a king and a palace is good for you. I am a saint and this hut is good for me."

The king was pensive for a while. When he spoke, he requested that the saint at least come to the palace when he begged for alms, and the saint agreed.

Upon returning to his palace, the king asked his queen to mix some gems with rice and be ready for the saintly beggar. When Purandardas came to the palace for alms, the queen gave him the special mixture, which the saint gave to his wife when he returned to his home.

That evening as his wife prepared the rice, she cried out in disgust, "My dear one, there are so many stones in this rice! This was from the palace!" She picked out the gems and discarded them outside. As agreed upon, Purandardas continued to beg at the palace, even though his wife was unhappy with the dirty rice.

Meanwhile the queen complained to the king that the great singer saint was a greedy person. "I have given him diamonds, pearls, and gold as you requested and now he is coming every day for this rice." The king became worried. His wife had raised doubt in his mind. He called the prime minister to consult with him.

The prime minister was undisturbed. "Please sir, this saint is not a greedy person. He is truly a saint. I will go and see what he is doing with the gold and gems."

When the prime minister arrived at the saint's hut, the wife was cleaning the rice and setting debris aside.

"What is in the rice?" He asked.

"Some stones," she replied. "I don't know why there are so many dirty stones in the rice. What can I do? I have to clean it."

"Where do you throw the debris?"

"Over there in that ditch," she said pointing outside the hut.

The prime minister went to the ditch and saw precious gems scattered about. He returned to the king and reassured him, "Really this is a divine couple. They have no use for diamonds, pearls, and gold. They only value rice because rice is food."

This story demonstrates the true meaning of detachment. A thing has value only when we have a demand for it. If we have no desire, nothing has value. If we have desire, then anything may be valuable to us. Desire creates value in worldly objects. Krishna indicates that a realized person sees a lump of clay, a stone, and gold as the same because they have the same material cause.[72] For a greedy person, everything has inflated value. When we withdraw the mind from the objects of the senses, then

---

[72] *Bhagavad Gītā* VI.8.

automatically the objects lose their value. This is detachment—not removing ourselves from the objects but removing our desire for them.

We must also analyze our concepts of heaven, the attainment of special powers, and the importance we place on our individual identity. We place a value on these subtle ideas because we fear mortality. The fear of mortality is an impression at the base of our individuation. We use ideas of heaven, attainments of powers, and inappropriate self-importance to pacify this fear. Stories of heaven create blind faith and encourage humankind to move away from truth.

Patañjali tells us not to seek happiness outside the self. When we are desireless, we gain detachment. Detachment comes by controlling our senses and mind. After steady, ongoing practice, we reach a desireless state and in this state, we realize pure consciousness in our own self.

~~~

I-16
tat param purusa-khyāter guna-vaitrsnyam
Perfect detachment, indifference to the *gunas*, comes when one realizes the self.

When we realize the seer is separate from the medium of nature, we are free from seeking happiness outside of the self. In perfect detachment, subtle experiences and worldly objects have no value for fulfilling our sense of self.

Krishna teaches, "The sense objects drop out for the abstinent person, though not the longing. Longing ceases completely when you intuit the supreme."[73] In the beginning stages of practice, we develop indifference toward objects of enjoyment. When we realize the seer as pure consciousness, objects lose all value. The treasure we seek exists within the self. The seer is intelligence, existence, and bliss. When we reach this stage, we truly understand that desire and attachment prompt us to value the external world. With this understanding, we can achieve the state of perfect detachment.

A stable intellect quiets the modifications of *chitta*, which purifies and stills this medium. Detachment provides the opportunity for experiencing the qualities of the seer and realizing these qualities as self. We become satisfied within our own self and realize that objects have a finite

---

[73] *Bhagavad Gīta* II.59.

usefulness in relation to our existence in this lifetime. Objects cannot bring us lasting satisfaction because desire for objects is never satisfied for more than a moment. The accumulation of objects does not bring sustained happiness. There is no end to the list of what we want tomorrow, next week, or next year. We plan, accumulate, and hold many things, making ourselves slaves to these objects. We squander our happiness for the mere hope of happiness. But when we understand the value of objects in relation to our real self, then we become the master of the objects.

Bliss is not an experience of the senses. Bliss is experienced through the wisdom of the intellect. It is a state of wellbeing independent of circumstances. Our cognitive senses, active senses, and mind are unable to realize this truth because they engage with the external world. They cannot turn inside. The senses can provide transitory pleasure, but our inner demand is for eternal happiness. The seer cannot be realized through the senses and mind. It is the subject of the intellect. The intellect is next to our real self. When we remove desire and doubt, we are stable and firm in our intellect.[74] In meditation the intellect keenly discriminates the seer from the seen.

Patañjali explains that it is not easy to realize the seer. We begin practice with detachment, and then with sustained, devoted effort, we realize the seer and free ourselves from attachment and suffering.

~~~

I-17
vitarka-vicārānandāsmitā-rūpānugamāt samprajñātah
**Stilling the modes of *chitta* sequentially in *vitarka* (gross form),
vicāra (subtle form), *ānanda* (blissfulness), and *asmitā*
(the sense of I-am) is called *samprajñātah samādhi*.**

Sāmkhya, a practice of analysis, encourages us to start from wherever we are and move up. We carefully analyze what we know and how we are attached, and gradually we climb to the highest level. *Samprajñātah* is perfect knowledge. The perfect knowledge we seek is of spirit and nature, the seer and the seen. In the stages of *samādhi*, we climb through our attachments with nature in order to reach the summit of causal nature and spirit. As we free ourselves from attachments, we see that the body is a projection of nature, and the seer is distinct from the modifications of *chitta*: the intellect, ego, and mind.

---

[74] *Bhagavad Gītā* II.68.

Patañjali discusses four stages of *samprajñātah samādhi*: *vitarka*, *vicāra*, *ananda*, and *asmitā*. *Vitarka* and *vicāra* are divided again into two categories that begin with the prefixes, *sa-* and *nir-*, meaning "with" and "without." Thus, *vitarka* becomes *savitarkā* and *nirvitarkā*, and *vicāra* becomes *savicāra* and *nirvicāra*. Because of these distinctions, the four stages of *samādhi* are discussed as six stages. These six levels are related with stilling the mind, ego, and intellect.

Patañjali expands on these stages in *sūtras* I-41 through I-51. A more thorough commentary is presented there.

Stages of *samprajñātah samādhi*	
savitarkā	Separate ego self from the gross body and physical world
nirvitarkā	Mind becomes free from attachments to physical objects as the identity of defining self with body and objects is released.
savicāra	Understand ego's association with desire related with need for self-importance and continuity and intellect's wrong notions, which propel the ego into activity.
nirvicāra	Ego relinquishes control to intellect. Modifications still.
ananda	Pure qualities of seer dawn within medium.
asmita	Qualities of seer established as individual sense of self.

Savitarkā and *nirvitarkā* are related with the mind. *Vitarka* means logic. In the stage of *savitarkā samādhi*, logic and analysis help us withdraw the mind and senses from the objects of senses and the physical world. The intellect is active, discriminating the real value and the nature of the body and objects of identification. Gradually, the mind is freed from attachments to the gross world and becomes more stable. When the mind and senses become quiet, this is *nirvitarkā*.

In *savicāra samādhi*, our focus shifts to understanding how the impressions and beliefs held in the intellect structure the identity of ego and propel the movement of ego into constant motion. By observing the movement of the ego, we gradually become aware of our beliefs. Our ideas about separation and limitation have fueled doubts and fears that drive the ego's activity. With keen discrimination we can ascertain the direct link between the ego and our beliefs and observe how changes in our beliefs

76

alter our behavior. *Savicārā* is the steady evaluation and analysis of our thoughts and beliefs that have led us into cycles of pleasure and loss.

As we become less externally active and more inwardly directed *nirvicārā* is reached. *Nirvicārā* is when the ego becomes quiet. Once the ego is no longer engaged and active with thoughts of the gross and subtle worlds, the intellect appears empty of projected form or identity. We have shifted from a body and ego centered reality, but have not become fully established in the seer or soul.

At this stage of *nirvicāra*, our knowledge of the three inner faculties of mind, ego and intellect is distinct. The mind and ego are free from the desire for enjoyment and automatically the intellect is pure. The intellect remains active with sharpened discrimination, but the modifications of *chitta* have been stilled. We realize how these faculties support an inner observer and we orient the intellect towards realizing the inner observer. This occurs in two stages: *ānanda* and *asmitā samādhi*.

With a pure intellect the *yogi* experiences the dawning light of the real self. This is called *ānanda samādhi*. The experience in this state is related with feelings of bliss, *ānanda*. Finally, one attains *asmitā samādhi*. *Asmitā* means I-am. Patañjali explains *asmitā* as the cognitive blending of the intellect and the seer. When both are present, I-am appears. In a pure intellect, I-am is related with its source in consciousness and the intellect is clearly known as an instrument of nature and the medium of consciousness.

In *sūtra* III-55, Patañjali states that emancipation is the result of purity of intellect and the seer. In the reflection of a pure intellect, the seer is known. In that state, we realize we are a projection of pure consciousness and we become one with that. We know, "I am That," indicating pure consciousness, and "not this," the intellect, the instrument of seeing. We realize "I am not the intellect, I am the seer." This is the meaning of the *mantra, soham. So* means "That;" *ham* means "I-am."

When we realize we are not the intellect, we become the master of the intellect. We realize the seer is the enlivener of *chitta* and the modifications—intellect, ego, and mind—are understood as instruments of the seer. I-am still exists. Individuation still exists. The ego has not been destroyed, but egoism or misidentification has been removed. The ego remains as long as the *chitta* is enlightened by consciousness, but it is no longer externally projected. Just as we clearly see our face reflected in a well-cleaned mirror, the real self is realized in a pure intellect. The self is the enlightener of the intellect. This state of realization is called *asmitā samādhi*.

Chitta shapes our individuation, not spirit or consciousness. Consciousness is one—absolute and infinite. Our *chitta* is a projection of the three *gunas*. Although spirit is one, different expressions appear in each individual due to the *chitta*. Each person has an individual *chitta* with specific impressions gathered from experience. Depending on our impressions, we have particular characteristics and tendencies. When we think of a person as divine, it is not due to spirit, but due to the purity of their intellect. Spirit is always one. The variation of our intellects causes individual characteristics, qualities, abilities, and behaviors. Diversity is the projection of nature, not spirit. Due to nature, spirit manifests in diverse forms.

~~~

I-18
virāma-pratyayābhyasa-pūrvah sanskāra-śeso 'nyah
When effort stops and only the impressions from this practice remain, that is *asamprajñātah samādhi* (seedless *samādhi*).

When we sit still to meditate, we stop the external activity of the body and senses. This does not automatically quiet the three inner instruments of mind, ego, and intellect. Gradually, the mind and ego quiet as they detach from the desire for gross and subtle experiences. With continued practice and determined detachment, eventually only the intellect is alert and present with the seer. In this state, the shadow of individuality is still cast by the medium of the *chitta*. A pure sense of "I-am" is reached where this seer is realized as independent from the fluctuations of intellect, ego, and mind. When this experience becomes established this is *samprajñātah samādhi*.

In the final stage of *asamprajñātah samādhi*, the seed of *chitta* is realized as producing the sense of I. Supreme detachment comes only when we realize the "I-am" is one with pure consciousness. This requires complete detachment from the medium itself, which is producing the sense of I. The Vedas describe this as a river flowing into the ocean. As the river merges into the ocean and becomes one with the ocean, in the same way a *yogi* realizes oneness.

Patañjali indicates that when all effort stops, the impressions of practice remain. The impressions of desire are gone. The intellect faces

78

inward and is not stimulated by external objects. In this final stage, the *yogi* knows that there is no duty, there is nothing to achieve, there is nothing further to realize, and there is nothing further to know. The intellect has fulfilled its purpose and effort ceases in a state of profound tranquility.[75] The intellect continues purely as an instrument of nature and spirit.

~~~

I-19
bhava-pratyayo videha-prakrti-layānām
**When those who are in subtle body take birth,
the thought of their previous level of *samādhi* takes them there.**

This *sutra* describes *yogis* in the matured stages of *ānanda* or *asmitā samādhi*. *Videha* refers to a *yogi* who has achieved *ānanda samādhi*. *Prakriti laya* describes a *yogi* who has reached *asmitā samādhi*. When *yogis* with this level of realization leave their bodies, they exist in subtle form in the divine realm, living as emancipated souls.[76] Individuation exists through the state of *asmitā samādhi*, the highest stage of *samprajñātaḥ samādhi*. Perfect detachment from the individual medium does not occur until the state of *asamprajñātaḥ samādhi*.

Even though these advanced *yogis*, referred to as *videha* and *prakriti laya*, reside in higher divine realms, they must take birth again to develop further. In this verse, Patañjali indicates that birth itself is all that is needed for them to achieve *asamprajñātaḥ samādhi*. When they take birth, memories and patterns rekindle to regain their previous position. Their dedication to practice in previous lives appears as virtue and inner stability. These come without effort because they are the results of previous practice, and the impressions of practice remain from life to life.

When *yogis* take birth, previous practice returns to them at some point without learning or studying. The knowledge they gained and their methods of practice spontaneously reemerge. Even the guru connects with them, because nature arranges the necessary means for them to continue on their path. For a *yogi* who achieves *asmitā samādhi*, birth is all that is needed to complete the journey. For those who attained *ānanda samādhi*, reading the truth contained in the scriptures leads to realization.

---

[75] *Yoga Sūtras* II-27.
[76] See also *Tattva Samāsa* 18.

Dedicated practitioners who have not yet attained the highest levels also experience the divine worlds when they leave their bodies.[77] They live there for some time according to their own motivation and virtue, but again they must take birth on the earth. Their births are advantageous. Krishna states: "They are born again in a pious family or in a family where *yogis* have come before." [78] Accordingly, these *yogis* are reborn among people of good character who are full of knowledge, thus awakening virtuous impressions that help them continue with their practice. Patañjali now describes the effort and qualities they need to move along the path.

~~~

I-20
śraddhā-vīrya-smrti-samādhi-prajñā-pūrvaka itaresām
In the case of others, detachment is preceded by faith, zeal, memory, evenness of intellect, and pure insight.

For other practitioners, detachment and *samādhi* come through continuing effort with faith, zeal, memory, stable intellect, and pure insight.

The heart of practice is *sraddhā*, faith. *Sraddhā* is established in a pure intellect, which is the foundation of deep faith. A pure intellect is doubtless. A doubting mind cannot trust or stay true to the path. Wisdom is the result of direct experience, which is very different from blind faith. *Sraddhā* is based on this wisdom. When the intellect is pure and perceives the light of pure consciousness, this direct experience establishes faith.

True devotion comes by facing hardship with determination. We learn to trust loving caregivers and teachers in order to grow and learn. Having faith in our teachers, we learn to read and write and discover the treasure of knowledge gathered by scholars. The sincere pursuit of knowledge guided by our teachers and scriptures deepens our faith and sustains our practice.

Vīrya, zeal or energy, is also necessary for practice. Zeal, energy and perseverance sustain higher practices. Practice is challenging. We have to control our senses, quiet our minds, and turn away from worldly enjoyment. Without effort and zeal, we will not succeed. If we postpone studying or working, we delay our success. Without zeal and firm faith, the higher practices of Yoga are out of our reach.

---

[77] See *Tattva Samāsa* 18.
[78] *Bhagavad Gītā* VI.41&42.

The third means for practice is *smriti*, that is, knowledge retained in memory. A persistent and continual practice keeps a lively and keen memory active for retaining knowledge. Ultimately, the memory of the seer during meditation is sustained in our daily lives. Yoga and Sāmkhya teach us that we are not far from truth, we are not separate from the seer, but we have forgotten. We have lost the memory of our real position. Practice and knowledge awaken our memory.

After deep faith, zeal, and memory come *samādhi* and *prajñā*. *Samādhi* is the development of a pure and even intellect. Our intellect becomes stable and pure as the *chitta* is stilled through meditation. Within a stable intellect, *prajñā* dawns, pure insight. Pure insight allows us to see the truth directly. This is stable wisdom.

~~~

I-21 and 22
tīvra-samvegānām āsannah
In the case of those who have ardent desire, *samādhi* is close.

mrdu-madhyādhimātratvāt tato pi viśesah
Even in ardent desire, there are three stages of soft, moderate, and intense, and with intense desire the achievement of *samādhi* is distinctive.

Patañjali now addresses the question of how quickly the highest levels of *samādhi* can be attained. He explains that success depends on the practitioner. The pace of success differs among those whose inner demand is mild (*mrdu*), moderate (*madhya*), or intense (*adhimātratvāt*). These three levels also have three subcategories of mild, moderate or intense, making a total of nine levels of intensity. For example, a mild practitioner may be weak and mild, moderately mild and mild with intensity. *Adhimātratvāt*, the most intense level, is referred to as *tivra*, energetic. Intense intensity is *tivra-tivra*. For those with intense desire, attainment is near.

Patañjali makes it clear that if we treat our practice as we would any ardent desire, the highest goal is quickly attained. But we are often sluggish, thinking, "Not today, maybe tomorrow." But tomorrow is never now, and the time for practice never comes. Only with ardent desire and firm determination can we control our minds and senses and achieve our goal.

If we have an ardent desire for the highest goal, we can immediately let go of all kinds of worldly affairs. A good analogy is the example of an arranged marriage as opposed to a marriage of choice. If a marriage is arranged and the woman is unfamiliar with her husband and his family, she is reluctant to leave her home. Another woman, who loves and chooses her husband, willingly leaves her family and other attachments for him. She is eager and doubtless. If we have determination to realize the seer, we willingly extricate ourselves from all other identities and distractions.

With devoted desire and detachment, we can achieve *samādhi*. Achievement demands practice, and to attain *samādhi* we have to train the intellect, ego, and mind. If we focus on this one destination, all of our endeavors will support our journey. What we are doing matters less than where we are going. Our goal gives meaning to our actions. Our intention drives our practice and our practice is sustained by the purity of our thoughts. But if our minds are not related with our highest destination, we walk in circles no matter what we do.

~~~

I-23
īsvara-pranidhānād vā
Or, *samādhi* is attained by surrendering to *Īsvara*.

Following the discussion of practice and detachment, which is emphasized in the teaching of Sāmkhya, Patañjali now introduces a second method of practice, *Īsvara pranidhāna*. The word *va* means "or," indicating a new topic.

Īsvara pranidhāna is the devotional practice of relating our individual soul with the universal soul. Comprehending the meaning of *Īsvara* and the formation of the individual soul is essential for this practice. This is not blind faith, but a spiritual science based on hypothesis and method. When Patañjali speaks of *Īsvara*, he explains that *Īsvara* is the source of life.

The *Chāndogya Upanishad* provides a discussion between a teacher and student regarding the source of life.

> In the beginning, my dear, there was "being" alone, one without a second. Some say in the beginning there was non-being alone; one without a second, and from that non-being, being was produced. But how, my dear, could it be thus? How could being be produced from non-being? On the contrary, my dear, in the beginning there was being alone, one without a second, and It thought, may I be many, may I grow forth. It cast forth fire...That fire cast forth water...That water sent forth food.

82

That divinity thought, let me enter into this by means of my living self and let me then develop names and forms. (*Chāndogya Upanishad* VI.2.1-4 & VI.2.2.2).

This Upanishad highlights the idea of the existence of a Supreme Being as the source of life from which a living self, the seer, emerges along with all names and forms, the seen. Both powers are phases of this highest Lord, *Īśvara*. The three attributes of the seen, *prakriti*, are indicated as fire, water and food. *Prakriti* is the material cause of this universe, that is to say all names and forms. The living self resides or co-exists with nature and is the inspiring force for nature to move and act.

The all-pervasive living self is called *ātman* and its presence within the individual medium of *chitta* is called *jivātman* or individual soul. Understanding and realizing that the *jivātman* is the presence of *ātman* is called devotion. Relinquishing the thought of separation and accepting this reality is surrender to the source of life.

This path is dictated more by the heart and emotion, but it is not without discrimination. The method teaches us to search beyond the limits of our self because whatever is limited cannot be the source of life. Patañjali teaches that the source must be the one, absolute, infinite cause of all. Whatever is changeable and related with diversity cannot be our cause. We use our intellect to understand this source, and then direct our effort towards unity. For many of us who are attached to the material world, it is difficult to concentrate on some abstract, formless entity.[79] Therefore, particularly at the initial stages of practice, fixing our minds on some personified form of *Īśvara* is easier.

On this path of devotion, we do not necessarily change the modes of action, but we modify our motives for performing action. Every initiative has a motive, and in the method of devotion, we perform our actions with a sacrificial attitude. We understand that this entire universe comes from the same source, and all of life and all beings participate in this divine expression. Acting in the service of divinity is the best way for an emotional person to purify his or her *chitta*. Changing the feeling behind an action converts action into worship and helps universalize the soul. Success in action is not the achievement of a goal; it is the continuity of effort while remembering divinity up to the last moment of life. Through

---

[79] *Bhagavad Gītā* XII.5.

the process of devotion, one gradually realizes that there is no difference between the individual soul and the universal self. They are both one.

~~~

I-24
klesa-karma-vipakāsayair aparāmrstah purusa-visesa īsvarah
Īsvara is a special kind of *purusha* untouched by *klesa* (misery), *karma* (action), *vipaka* (result), and *āsayaih* (the accumulation of *karma*).

When the Supreme Being manifests, both the living self and the three attributes of nature appear in causal form. Patañjali describes this first formation as *purusha-visesa*, a special kind of *purusha* called Īsvara. The universe is projected from this singular form. Therefore, Īsvara is called the supreme source.

Īsvara is described here as a special kind of *purusha* untouched by misery, actions, outcomes and impressions.[80] Īsvara is a pure, untainted medium, whereas each individual *chitta* progresses through an evolutionary process influenced by actions and suffering.

Patañjali indicates that Īsvara is not far from us. In fact, we are inseparable from our source. We are intimately connected to this source as rays of light are all part of the sun. The individual soul is the presence of the universal soul in our individual medium providing us a personal, immanent experience of our source. Īsvara is the abode of blissfulness, and our souls are expressions of that universal soul. Because of this innate oneness, we long for the experience of blissful wholeness. Every effect is part of its cause, and every effect will one day merge back into its cause. Our inner longing is to be one with our source.

We can understand this inner demand through an analysis of our bodies' needs. Our bodies need warmth. As the element of fire warms the body, we become thirsty. Thirst reminds us of our body's need for the element of water. We feel hungry because our bodies need earthly elements for metabolism, cleansing and building. We need to breathe to nourish and flush our cells. Our breath moves the element of air in and out of our bodies. And our bodies require the element of space. We cannot function without space in our joints for movement or the vacuum in our lungs for breathing. Our bodies are a combination of these five

---

[80] See *Yoga Sūtras* II-3 through 9 for explanation of *klesa*, and II-12 through 15 for a discussion of *karma*.

primordial elements: space, air, fire, water, and earth. The natural demands of the body lead us to the five elements that are the material cause of the physical body.[81]

The same process applies to our understanding of *Īśvara*. We feel an inner demand for immortality, for perfection, and for knowledge. These needs reveal the essence of our cause: immortality, perfection, and omniscience. *Īśvara* is the name of this cause, often called God, the source for which we long. What is most important is that as thirst indicates the presence of water in our body, the demand for truth, knowledge, and infinity indicates the presence of God within us because these are the qualities of divinity. This logic can help us understand, seek, and realize the presence of the divine within us.

~~~

I-25
tatra niratiśayam sarvajñatva-bījam
There in *Īśvara*, the seed of omniscience is incomparable.

Because of our identification with the body and senses, we think that the cause of life is nature and the primordial elements. Nature is the source of our body, but not the source of our soul. Nature is without knowledge and sentience. Knowledge and consciousness are not properties of nature, but of soul. And the soul is of *Īśvara*--the source of all knowledge and consciousness.

The knowledge of *Īśvara* cannot be compared to any level of human knowledge. And yet, *Īśvara* is knowable. We are all sparks of *Īśvara's* illuminating knowledge. *Īśvara* is infinite knowledge and infinite knowledge is *Īśvara*. Knowledge is not a separate part, quality, virtue, or property; infinite knowledge is *Īśvara*. In the *Rāmāyana* of Tulsidas,[82] we read, "Whatever we are seeing of light in the world, that light is only a little spark, nothing else. Sunlight, moonlight, starlight, and firelight are nothing but divine sparks. And He is the light of lights." *Isvara* is the enlightener of all, the source of all wisdom, residing in each of us in the care of our intellect.

~~~

---

[81] See *Tattva Samāsa* 3. The five primordial elements are part of the sixteen modifications of nature and form the gross world. See also *Yoga Sūtras* II-19.
[82] Tulsidas (1532-1623), wrote the epic *Rāmāyana, Shri Rāmacharitamānasa.*

I-26

sa pūrvesām api guruh kālenānavacchedāt
That (*Īśvara*), unlimited by time, is also the teacher of ancients.

Īśvara is the teacher of teachers. Anyone who has realized true knowledge has gained it from *Īśvara*. In the Upanishads we find, "He who is giving birth in the beginning, who is father of the creative power, and who has poured knowledge in him, surely we are praying to that supreme source who is the bestower of knowledge in the first being. May he enlighten our intellects and may we be surrendered to him."[83]

We cannot easily learn without teachers. When students have a trusted and beloved teacher, they are eager to learn and learn quickly. Knowledge cannot be bought; it must be sought. Knowledge is gained through a teacher, and there is an eternal teacher, one eternal guru. The eternal guru is omniscient and omnipresent.

Īśvara is beyond time, space, and relativity. *Īśvara* is eternal, all-pervasive, omnipresent and omnipotent. He is beyond suffering, action, the results of action, and the abode of all action. There is no time, place or circumstances in our life when we are without *Īśvara*. Only God is like God and cannot be compared to any other thing.

~~~

I-27

tasya vācakah pranavah
The designator of *Īśvara* is *Om*

Here, Patañjali teaches that we can know God, reach God and surrender to God through the sound of *Om*. *Om* is the un-struck, untouched, primordial sound.

Normally when we create sound, we touch the tongue to various parts of the mouth. This divine sound of *Om* is created without touching any part of the tongue to the mouth. At the end of the sound, the tongue presses up against the palate, which extends the sound rather than stopping it. This natural, continuous, divine sound indicates the supreme cause.

When we are ready to surrender to the infinite, we can surrender through this sound. It is a vehicle for our soul. In the Upanishads, we find

---

[83] *Svetāsvatara Upanishad* VI-18.

the image of a bow and arrow to describe the chanting *Om*.[84] When we draw an arrow with a bow, aim with skill, and then shoot, the arrow finds and enters its target. In the same way, the sound of *Om* is like the bow, the soul is the arrow, and *Īśvara* is the destination. When we draw breath into the base *chakra*, *mūlādhāra*, it is like pulling the arrow back on the bow. When we pull the arrow back well, it soars to its destination.

Anāhat describes the un-struck nature of *Om*. *Hāt* means touched. No sounds are created without tapping or striking the tongue against the teeth or the palate. Striking, *hāt*, creates all kinds of sound, including water hitting stones, hands tapping drums, or fingers strumming a guitar. Sounds are made with touch. The divine sound of *Om* is made without striking, *anāhat*. This sound is related with our breath, *prāna*. In this verse, the term that designates *Om* is *pranavah*. *Om* is related with our breath alone.

The mystical sound of *Om* has three sounds within it, written with the three letters AUM. The A sound begins at the base in the *mūlādhāra*, moves up the spine through the *sushumnā* on U, and merges into the top of the head in the *brahma chakra* on M. M is not a labial sound produced by the lips, but is more of an -ng sound created by pressing the tongue upward toward the palate. There is no final consonant.[85]

~~~

I-28
taj-japas tad-artha-bhāvanam
The repetition of that name with the feeling of its meaning is surrender to *Īśvara*.

When we inhale all the way to the base of our spine and send the breath up through the spinal cord to the top of the head, we feel the sound touching our *brahma chakra*. To experience this, sit calmly, turn the mind inside, and gradually extend the breath. Add the sound of *Om* on a long exhale, reaching toward the top of the head. *Omkāra*, the chanting of *Om*, is not creating sound with the mouth, but with our breath. When our breath passes through the *sushumnā*, the energetic channel in the spinal cord, and rises to touch this highest place, this is called *pranavah*, the process of our *prāna* rising and joining *Īśvara* with breath and sound.

---

[84] *Mundaka Upanishad* II.2.4
[85] See the appendix of *The Eternal Soul* by Brahmrishi Vishvatma Bawra for the explanation of *Om* from the *Māndūkya Upanishad*.

When our *prāna* elevates with *Om* into *brahma chakra*, our breath and thought are focused there. When we realize the meaning of *Om* as we create the sound, our individual soul joins with *Īsvara*. *Om* is the vibration of one, absolute, infinite consciousness. Patañjali teaches that if you repeat the sound of *Om*, you will rise into the presence of God.

The *Katha Upanishad* explains that the Supreme cannot be obtained through the senses nor through speech, mind, or vision. It is comprehended by that practitioner who realizes the supreme existing within as his or her own self. Those who trust that the supreme does exist and can be realized, to them the Lord is revealed. They will achieve immortality and becomes filled with divinity.[86]

~~~

I-29

tatah pratyak-cetnādhigamo 'pyantarāyābhāvaś ca
From that comes the attainment of inward-directed consciousness, and also the disappearance of blocks.

Pratyak cetana refers to *jivātmā*, the individual soul. This indweller enlivens our bodies and enables us to have awareness. By slowly reciting *pranavah* with breath, our mind and consciousness become centered in the *brahma chakra* where our individual soul meets *Īsvara*. Through devotion we become established in the self and gradually the obstacles on our path of Yoga are diminished.

This practice helps us move inward. The sound withdraws our energy and focus from outside as we awaken inside. By realizing the meaning, we develop stability in the intellect that guides us in our daily lives. Our misidentifications, infatuations and attachments weaken as we shift our attention from an external focus to the source of our life. *Om* produces an experience of unity free from comparison. As we move toward *samādhi*, becoming established in the source of self, we are internally satiated and our desire for external fulfillment gradually wanes.

~~~

---

[86] *Katha Upanishad* 2.3.9, 2.3.12&13.

I-30

vyādhi-styāna-sanśaya-pramādālasyāvirati-bhrānti-darśanālabdha-
bhūmikatvānavasthitatvāni citta-vikṣepās te 'ntarāyāḥ
**Physical disease, lethargy, negligence, doubt, laziness, a lack of
detachment, misconception, non-achievement of any stage of
samādhi, and lack of stability with experience gained—these
are the obstacles on the path that disrupt the *chitta*.**

Patañjali describes a total of fourteen obstacles that cause us to
stumble. The wrong impressions we hold in our *chitta* manifest in various
forms, including obstacles to our practice. In this aphorism Patañjali
identifies nine.

Physical disease interrupts the physical practices of *āsana, prāṇāyāma,*
mudrā and *bandha,* making it impossible to sit with integrity for meditation.

The remaining eight obstacles in this *sūtra* are mental and intellectual.
Dullness, doubt, lethargy, laziness, and lack of detachment are mental
obstacles. Misconception, failure to reach a stage of *samādhi,* and a lack of
stability are intellectual obstacles. These obstacles arise in a disturbed and
impure *chitta,* which is the effect of *rajoguna* and *tamoguna.*

Krishna states, "The faith of embodied beings is of three kinds: *sattvic,*
rajasic, or *tamasic.* Humankind is made of faith. Whatever faith he has, thus
he is."[87] Our beliefs manifest in our lives. If our *chitta* is *sattvic,* it is pure
and free from the intellectual diseases of delusion, infatuation, and
misperception. When *sattoguna* prevails in the intellect, the mental diseases
of lust, greed, anger, attachment, passion, pride, and hypocrisy, which are
caused by *rajoguna,* are not active; also the *tamasic* diseases of lethargy,
laziness and countless other physical diseases are subdued.

~~~

I-31

duhkha-daurmanasyāṅgam-ejayatva-śvāsa-praśvāsā vikṣepa
sahabhuvah
**Pain, depression, body trembling, uncontrolled long inhalation,
and uncontrolled exhalation accompany the obstacles.**

The remaining five obstacles are pain, depression, trembling of the
body, and uncontrolled inhalation and exhalation of breath. It is difficult
to practice while these obstacles are present. *Duhkha* means pain. If we are

---

[87] *Bhagavad Gītā* XVII.2&3.

deeply in pain from grief, we cannot meditate. People say that when we suffer we call God. This is not true. It is difficult to focus on anything when we are deeply distracted by pain. Suffering may turn us toward practice, but the suffering itself is not practice.

After pain, Patañjali lists depression. Depression overpowers the mind. In this state the mind is overwhelmed by hopeless lethargy. A depressed person is dying in a living state. Depression often gives rise to physical illness and sometimes to suicide. It is a debilitating experience.

Trembling comes when the mind is not stable. When we sit for meditation with an unstable mind, the body fidgets disturbing our practice.

Breathing is uncontrolled when we are angry, lustful, fearful, or greedy. Our energy depends on our breath. When our breath is uncontrolled, we lose life energy. Krishna states, "The threefold gateway of hell that destroys the pure self is made of lust, anger and greed. One should try to remove them."[88] If we want to sustain our life energy and build stamina, we must control our emotions and save our breath.

~~~

I-32
tat-pratisedhārtham eka-tattvābhyāsah
In order to prevent these obstacles, a one-pointed practice is necessary.

To prevent these obstacles from interfering with our practice, the mind needs a one-pointed focus. This is achieved through meditation. In this *sūtra*, Patañjali uses *abhyāsa*, which means practice or effort. We should practice focusing the mind. Gradually, as we are able to fix the mind for longer periods of time, we gain mastery.

The phrase *eka-tattva* has two meanings. The first meaning is one-pointed focus. The second refers to *Īśvara* as the one supreme principal. In meditation and our daily life, we should always remember our existence is part of *Īśvara*. In *sūtra* I-28, Patañjali recommends the one-pointed practice of chanting *Om* while meditating on its meaning. In *sūtras* I-33 through I-39, Patañjali teaches additional practices for gaining a one-pointed focus. Different traditions of Yoga emphasize various practices. A settled mind is the foundation for a deeper practice. There are multiple ways to train the mind to become focused and calm.

---

[88] *Bhagavad Gītā* XVI.21.

~~~

I-33
maitrī-karunā-muditopeksānām sukha-duhkha-punyāpunya-visayānām bhāvanātas citta prasādanam.
Purity and happiness are maintained by practicing friendliness with happy people, compassion with suffering people, gladness with virtuous people, and indifference toward vicious people.

We may be eager to focus our minds but living in society challenges our practice. To support our practice while interacting with others, Patañjali describes four categories of human beings: the happy, the suffering, the virtuous and the vicious. There are so few people who lead a happy life, while the numbers of people who suffer are countless. Those who are spiritual, gentle, helpful and selfless are virtuous or divine. Cruel, selfish, or vicious people are demonic.[89]

Patañjali suggests four attitudes: friendliness, compassion, gladness and indifference. When others are happy, we should be friendly with them not jealous. Jealousy in the presence of others' success and happiness drags us away from practice. With those who are suffering, he advises compassion. Compassion is the gateway to divinity. We should try to help people who are suffering, offering them empathy and providing practical help.

We should be inspired and glad to be with a virtuous person. We naturally rejoice in the presence of someone who is uplifting. Cruel and selfish people have a very different effect on us. Patañjali suggests indifference toward vicious people. If we befriend them, they will lead us astray, and if we make them our enemy, we suffer from aversion and anger. We should avoid destructive people and be neutral toward them if we must be in their company.

~~~

I-34
pracchardana-vidhāranābhyām vā prānasya
Or you can prevent those obstacles through the practice of exhaling and holding out the breath.

This breathing practice helps control the modes of *chitta*. *Pracchardana* means exhaling and *vidhārana* means holding out. Careful practice is

---

[89] Krishna divides humanity into two categories: "There are two classes of beings in this world, the divine and the demonic." *Bhagavad Gītā* XVI.6.

necessary to learn how to retain the breath outside. Holding the breath out is beneficial once the body is prepared through vigorous deep breathing called *bhastrikā prānāyama*. *Bhastrikā* is a powerful practice that purifies our gross, subtle and causal bodies. These practices require a pure diet and a moderate life style.

If we relate *prānāyama* practice with *mantra*, we purify the body, mind, and intellect. When we develop our capacity for *prānāyama*, our minds become stable for sitting in prolonged meditation. The Upanishads tell us that if we moderate our breath, we can subdue our mind.[90] Patañjali teaches more about *prānāyama* in *sūtras* II-49 through 53.

~~~

I-35
visayavatī vā pravrttir utpannā manasah sthiti-nibandhanī
Also, the stability of mind can be gained by experiencing the subtle elements.

According to Sāmkhya, the subtle vibrations within the gross elements are the *tanmātras*: sound, touch, form, taste, and smell. By focusing our mind on these subtle qualities, we internalize our experience. This brings the senses and mind away from external objects and develops an inward focus. With refined guidance and firm dedication, we can stabilize the mind through this practice.

~~~

I-36
visokā vā jyotismatī
Or by experiencing stability of mind that is light and free of anxiety.

Visoka means without anxiety. In this method of concentration, we put our minds on a particular object or point. For example, we focus on a dot in the center of different colors. At first, we see all the colors and the dot. As practice continues, the mind becomes fixed on the dot, which becomes luminous. When we are able to focus in this way, the mind settles and is free of anxiety.

~~~

---

[90] *Svetasvatara Upanishad* II.9.

I-37
vītarāgaviṣayam vā cittam
Or by contemplating on a person who is perfectly detached.

The mind takes the shape of whatever it focuses on. Contemplation of a perfectly detached person brings that person's qualities close. Throughout history, people have meditated on their gurus. Success with this method depends on the purity of the guru's wisdom. If the guru is detached, the disciple develops detachment, but if the guru is not detached, the practitioner does not benefit from this practice.

This is a great method, and it does not depend on having a guru. Any saintly person can be the focus of this practice. There are many divine people in all traditions and all faiths. It is very difficult for the mind to fix on an abstract idea of divinity. It is much easier to fix the mind on a great *yogi* or a divine person.

~~~

I-38
svapna-nidrā-jñānālambanam vā
Or by remembering the knowledge of dream and sleep states.

The knowledge gained in dreams and deep sleep also helps the mind become one-pointed. Remembering a dream can lead us toward meditation. If we dream of being with God, or if we see a divine form in a dream, we can meditate on that subtle experience. According to scriptures, the vision of a divine person in a dream is divine grace. Dwelling on this blessing in meditation uplifts us and internalizes our focus.

In deep sleep, we are thoughtless and we receive energy. We lose energy during our waking state, sometimes to the point of exhaustion. In deep sleep, the ego and the mind quiet and energy is restored. Patañjali suggests contemplating the state of deep sleep. When we meditate on this state we quiet ourselves and rejuvenate the body.

Ramana Maharshi was a saint who, at the age of 13, spontaneously meditated on death. Someone had died in his neighborhood, and he went to where people were gathering. He gazed at the dead man, who was lying on the ground with his legs apart and his hands open. Ramana Maharishi decided to experiment by placing his own body in this position. He went to the roof of his house, lay down on his back, and dwelt on death. While lying there, his consciousness rose and he went into *samādhi*.

Ramana Maharshi had not told anyone of his experiment, and when evening came his family could not find him. They were upset and reported him missing to the police.

After three days, a woman went to the roof to spread her clothes to dry. She saw the boy and thought he was dead. The family gathered and they could not find any signs of life. Shortly after the commotion, Ramana Maharshi started breathing again. A few hours later, he began to stir. When he returned to full consciousness, he told his family about his experiment.

"I just came up on the roof to think about how people die, and then experienced death. The state was blissful." He decided to continue with this practice. Eventually he became a well-known teacher.

~~~

I-39
yathābhimata-dhyānād vā
Or by focusing on whatever is most dear to us.

We can also make the mind one-pointed by meditating on something that is dear to us. If we think deeply about devoting our whole life to one purpose, we gain a one-pointed focus.

There is a story of a farmer and his buffalo that illustrates this method. The farmer went to learn meditation from a *yogi*. The *yogi* instructed him to stay inside a room at the ashram for forty days. Milk was brought to his door and was his only nourishment. The farmer was instructed not to speak, but to chant a specific *mantra*.

The farmer's buffalo was very precious to him. While he chanted the *mantra*, he naturally kept his bull in his mind. After forty days, the guru called to the farmer, who was in a state of deep contentment. The guru asked him to come out of the room.

The farmer hesitated, saying "I cannot come out; my horns will not fit through the door."

The guru went inside and pushed the farmer through the door. As the farmer fell out of the room, the force of his fall elevated his concentrated *prāna* and he went into *samādhi*. His single pointed focus on the bull quieted his mind and prepared him for an experience of *samādhi*.

~~~

I-40

paramāṇu-parama-mahattvānto 'sya vaśīkāraḥ
Mastery is when the stabilized mind reaches from the subtle to the vast.

When we can stabilize our mind on the subtlest point, we can understand how everything emerges from this causal seed. In yoga, *Īśvara* is the source of this universe, the causal form. *Īśvara* is indicated by many names, but as the source of the projected, expanding universe it is known as *Hiraṇyagarbha* or the cosmic egg. From this most subtle point, the vast universe expanded. When we comprehend *Īśvara* our understanding reaches from the subtle to the vast.

Patañjali states that by fixing the mind on the causal level of nature, we simultaneously realize the vastness of this universe. In *A Short History of Nearly Everything*, Bill Bryson presents the scientific view of how the vast universe originates from a subtle "singularity."

> No matter how hard you try you will never be able to grasp just how tiny, how spatially unassuming a proton is. Now imagine shrinking that down to a billionth of its normal state and adding a tiny ounce of matter to it. You are now ready to start a universe.

> It is natural but wrong to visualize this singularity as a kind of pregnant dot hanging in a dark, boundless void. But there is no space, no darkness. The singularity has no "around" around it. There is no space for it to occupy, no place for it to be. We can't even ask how long it has been there—whether it has been there forever, quietly waiting for the right moment. Time doesn't exist. There is no past for it to emerge from.

> Outside the singularity there is no where. When the universe begins to expand, it won't be spreading out to fill a larger emptiness, the only space that exists is the space it creates as it goes. From nothing, our universe begins.

> In a single blinding pulse, a moment of glory too swift and expansive for any form of words, the singularity assumes heavenly dimensions, space beyond conception. In the first lively second is produced gravity and other forces that govern physics. There is a lot of heat now, enough to begin the nuclear reactions that create the lighter elements—principally hydrogen and helium, with a dash of lithium. In three minutes, 98 percent of all the

matter there is or will ever be has been produced. We have a universe.[91]

In Yoga, the universe not only expands from this singularity, *Īśvara*, but also abides inside and outside every living being as the conscious soul of the cosmos. We grasp this most subtle and vast experience through our *chitta*. In the *Svetasvatara Upanishad*, we read that the *chitta* is both profoundly small, yet capable of holding infinity. The hymn compares its size to $1/10,000^{th}$ of a hair's width.[92] With a refined internal focus, we can reach this finest medium of causal nature and experience the infinite universal soul.

~~~

I-41
ksīna-vrtter abhijātasyeva maner grahītr-grahana-grāhyesu
tat-stha-tad-ānjanatā samāpattih

Having attenuated the modes of *chitta*, the *chitta* appears to take on the features of the focus of meditation, whether it be the knower, the instrument of knowing, or the object known, as does a crystal. This identification or engrossment is called *samāpatti*.

To begin a deeper practice of meditation, we must make the mind one-pointed. A singular focus withdraws the mind from outer identity and stimulation, attenuating the modes of *chitta*. This prepares us for the inner work of realizing the source of self. To prepare us for inner practice, Patañjali explains the natural position and properties of *chitta*.

Patañjali compares the *chitta* to a clear, pure crystal jewel. Although the jewel is clear, it appears to be colorful when a colorful object is placed next to it. Many colors can be seen in a crystal, but these colors are not its property. The colors are simply nearby and reflecting through it. This type of receptivity is called *asya*. When we remove the colorful object, the original purity of the crystal is known.

As a crystal has the ability to adopt all reflections, the *chitta* is able to adopt and reflect countless modifications or *vrittis*. The *chitta* is originally without modifications. It is primarily the projection of *sattoguna*, light, but because it is a projection of nature, all three *gunas* are present. *Chitta* is the first projection of nature, and in its pure state, it is untainted and without

---

[91] *A Short History of Nearly Everything*, page 9-10.
[92] *Svetasvatara Upanishad* V-9.

distortions. When worldly objects or experiences reflect in it, then impressions appear in the *chitta*. Like a crystal, the *chitta* holds the qualities of the objects and experiences that are brought close. Identification of the self with these external qualities pollutes the *chitta*. Removing these impressions returns the *chitta* to purity.

When the *chitta* is pure, it captures the features of the object of meditation. In devotional practices, *Īśvara* is the object of meditation. *Īśvara* is the abode of intelligence, existence and bliss. *Īśvara* is the knower of all, the abode of knowledge, and the cause of this infinite diverse expression, all that can be known. In a deeper practice of meditation, we realize and identify our individual self with the object of meditation; we become absorbed in or engrossed with *Īśvara*.

As discussed in I-23, when this universe manifests from *Īśvara*, an all-pervasive living self called *ātman*, soul, pervades this projected universe. When the presence of this universal soul is within the individual medium of *chitta* it is called *jivātman* or individual soul. Understanding and realizing that the *jivātman* is the presence of *ātman* is called devotion. Relinquishing the thought of separation and accepting this reality is engrossment in the source of life. This realization of unity is Yoga.

Over many lifetimes of experience, we have formed beliefs about our existence. Primary is a belief that we are separate from our source. Instead of understanding how the *chitta* adopts and produces an immanent, personal experience of *Īśvara*, we have come to accept and believe our existence is separate and individual. We adopt the quality of the medium as the form of our existence, rather than the qualities of *Īśvara* appearing as a seer or knower within us.

The difference between this devotional method and the method of practice and detachment is in our attitude. In practice and detachment, we detach from the objects and instruments of nature because they are not the seer. In this method, we understand the gross, subtle, and causal unfoldment of nature as the expression of *Īśvara*; they are gifts of God. The body, mind and ego are recognized as transitory but valuable instruments of service. The intellect is a powerful tool of discrimination, which guides our lives. *Jivātman*, I-amness, is the means for experiencing an intimate personal relationship with *Īśvara*. I-amness is the gateway. As we develop proficiency in service, the *chitta* is gradually purified.

In this devotional section the stages of realizing *Īśvara* are called engrossment, *samāpatti*. Similar to the development of *samprajñatah* and *asamprajñātah samādhi*, *samāpatti's* development is described as being with seed, *sabij* and without seed, *nirbij*. Our identity is with the seed of the medium or rises above the seed and is fully established in *Īśvara*. The development is from "I-am this and that," egoistic self, to I-amness, *jivātman*, and finally into a state of absorption, "amness alone," *Īśvara*.

Sabij samādhi separates the individual soul from gross and subtle identifications. Gradually, as we discriminate and detach from the physical world and the senses, the ego relinquishes its control and accepts the guidance of the intellect. Then the qualities of *Īśvara* begin to dawn within us, yet the influence of the individual seed, *chitta*, continues an individual experience, *jivātman*, I-amness. Further discrimination is needed to rise above the seed and experience absorption into *Īśvara*. As a drop of rain enters into the ocean, we experience that our individual soul is part and parcel of *Īśvara*. This state, *nirbij*, is without the seed of individual identity.

~~~

I-42
tatra śabdārtha-jñāna-vikalpaih sankīrnā savitarkā samāpattih
Savitarkā samāpatti (engrossment) is where the word, the meaning or the knowledge is pointed at alternatively.

Vitarkā means logic, and in this stage, logic or analysis is used. Objects can be known in three ways: by name or with words, by the meaning or purpose of the object, and finally by knowledge. *Sabda* indicates the name, *artha* refers to the meaning, and *jñāna* is the knowledge of both name and form. When all three are related with one point, it is called *savitarkā samāpatti*.

In the early stages of meditation, our minds are not stable. We have many distracting thoughts. This first stage of realization begins with a careful observation and assessment of our thoughts.

We can understand this process by examining our identification with the body. First, we concentrate the mind, purposefully drawing our consciousness inside. Once the mind is focused, we analyze the temporal nature of the body, knowing that it will die and these elements will disperse. This analysis weakens our attachment to the body. With this practice, we initate a deep inquiry into what is nature and what is soul. By using our reasoning to seek the undying self, we gradually uplift identification from the body and senses.

In this practice, the focus of the cognitive senses is diverted from the external world and centered in the mind. We experience resistance to change because we believe we will gain happiness from the material world. The mind's resistance to concentration arises in the form of questions, objections and distractions. Since we have found enjoyment in objects and relationships, and also disappointment, the question arises, "What is enjoyment?" Scriptures and teachers explain that enjoyment is related to having and holding objects in conditions that are acceptable to us. Yet happiness is a state of wellbeing not dependent on objects but residing in the soul. This knowledge deepens our search.

Vitarkā is withdrawing the senses from their objects and analyzing the actual qualities and value of objects. In *vitarkā*, we alternately contemplate the name of the object, the meaning of the object, and knowledge about the object, gaining perspective and freeing ourselves from gross attachments. When we focus our awareness on one point and think on it again and again, the mind stops moving hither and thither, and we reach *samāpatti*. With a one-pointed focus, correct knowledge is attained and the mind quiets and becomes stable. This process of concentration is *savitarkā samāpatti*.

~~~

I-43
smrti-pariśuddhau svarūpa-śūnyevārtha-mātra-nirbhāsā nirvitarkā
When the knower leaves the previous memory behind, and also his own awareness, and becomes one with the object, that engrossment is called *nirvitarkā*.

Nirvitarkā is without the activity of reasoning. The meaning and value we have held and projected onto an object stops. *Svarūpa śūnyeva* means seemingly empty of form. We dissolve our attachments with the gross object, and the object stands alone without forming our false identity. We are able to concentrate on the object alone without superimposing value and meaning upon it.

Nirvitarkā occurs when we determine that happiness and enjoyment do not lie in our external identification and attachments. We experience detachment. Our identity is no longer formed by the attendant modifications related with the object.

~~~

I-44
etayaiva savicārā nirvicārā ca sūksma-visayā vyākhyātā
**With the explanation of the previous two (*savitarkā* and
nirvitarkā), *savicārā* and *nirvicārā,* whose objects are
subtle, have been explained.**

Patañjali explains that in a manner similar to *savitarkā* and *nirvitarkā*, we continue to use logic and analysis in *savicārā* and *nirvicārā*. But now the focus shifts from gross attachments to subtle attachments. The internal functions of intellect, ego and mind are studied to understand the subtle impressions that drive our attachments.

In the early stages of meditation, our minds are not stable. We have many distracting thoughts. This first stage of realization begins with a careful observation and assessment of our thoughts.

Previously, we learned that over lifetimes of experience we have formed the belief that our existence is separate from its source. This feeling of separation has produced a sense of lack, creating an inner demand for wholeness. By externalizing this demand, we have formed many attachments to the world, leading us further and further away from our source. The compulsion to accumulate objects and ideas has confounded our identity.

During the first two stages of meditation, we shift our identification away from the body and the objects of senses. But craving and hankering remain. This leads to a growing awareness that it is not the object itself, but something more subtle that causes craving. Our search for that cause leads us closer to satisfying the inner demand for emancipation.

As mentioned, *chitta* is the abode of our beliefs called impressions. These impressions form our ability to discriminate and make judgments, the function of the intellect. Patañjali describes the intellect as the instrument of seeing and explains that when the seer is blended with this instrument, an egoistic self called *asmitā* is produced.[93] The two distinct powers of the seer and the intellect are blended into one individual identity.

What we value and hold in our intellect is revealed by the mind. The mind is nothing but waves of thought. In deeper states of awareness, we see our thoughts defining how our ego engages with the external world. We come to observe the mind as the movement of the ego. *Savicārā*

---

[93] *Yoga Sūtras* II-6.

engrossment is the process of understanding these subtle inner functions of mind, ego and intellect.

Our ego expresses in patterns of behavior that lead us toward what we like and away from our aversions. The ego includes our skills and the capacity to achieve what we want and protect ourselves from what we do not want near us. It is the form of our innate nature and inherent dispositions. The active attribute of nature, *rajoguna*, is predominant in ego as it is a performer or agent of action.

Our egoistic self is the abode of desire, which is insatiable. It dwells on attaining pleasures and comforts. These include subtle relationships, objects, powers, heavenly places, and self-importance. The ego hankers for power and continuity of existence. It wants to dominate to create its preferences. The ego acts to satisfy our need to feel complete and connected.

By observing the movement of the ego, we gradually become aware of our beliefs. Our ideas about separation and limitation have fueled doubts and fears that drive the ego's activity. With keen discrimination we can ascertain the direct link between the ego and our beliefs and observe how changes in our beliefs alter our behavior. *Savicāra* is the steady evaluation and analysis of our thoughts and beliefs that have led us into cycles of pleasure and loss. The dependency on favorable conditions is attendant with anxiety and fear of loss. Repeatedly as we encounter disturbances in our relationships with family and society, we can gradually discern that the dramas emerge from our own seed misconceptions held in the intellect.

A desire for improvement prompts us to seek inner happiness and we redirect our efforts toward gaining more knowledge and awareness. Gradually the ego aligns itself with this new direction, shifts away from emotionally reactive behaviors, and relinquishes control to the the intellect. We become more thoughtful and observant as our lives are governed by discrimination and free will.

Our knowledge of these three inner faculties of mind, ego and intellect deepens and we see how they support an inner observer. A pure intellect is capable of discriminating between what we ought to do or ought not to do. The ego guided by the intellect acts skillfully, motivated by service. The mind displays the information of the cognitive and actives senses while also receiving the promptings of the ego and the values of the intellect. A one-pointed focus stills these modifications of *chitta* and orients them toward the inner observer. As we become less externally active and more inwardly directed *nirvicāra* is reached, but our analysis is not complete until we find the seer.

~~~

I-45
sūksma-visayatvam cālinga-paryavasānam
Subtlety pertaining to objects extends to *alinga*, the unmanifest.

Through careful observation and keen analysis, we reach the point of understanding the seen. Patañjali explains in *sūtra* II-18 that the seen—the three attributes of light, movement and stability—projects into the elements and senses, and is for experience and emancipation. Continuing in II-19 he states that the three gunas appear in four stages: formless (*alingam*), causal (*lingam*), subtle (*avisesa*), and gross (*visesa*).

Visesa, the gross level, includes the mind, the five cognitive senses, the five active senses and the five primordial elements. *Avisesa* includes ego and the five *tanmātras*: sound, touch, form, taste and smell. *Chitta*, the first projection of nature, is indicated by *lingam*, which means mark. It is also the place of the intellect. *Alinga* is beyond the seen, but is the source of the seen. According to Sāmkhya, there is one pure root cause of all manifested forms called *prakriti. Prakriti* is the three *gunas*, which are the unmanifest causal phenomenon of this universe. They are invisible and imperceptible but are known by their effects. Causal nature is understood by inference and testimony and not by observation.[94]

The *tanmātras* are the five subtle elements which produce the five gross elements. All gross form, including our body, is only an accumulation of the five primordial elements. The faculties are thirteen: the five active senses, the five cognitive senses, the mind, the ego, and the intellect. Our active senses, working through the body, engage with the physical world. The cognitive senses collect the subtle stimuli of sound, touch, form, taste and smell. The information from both active and cognitive senses is displayed in the mind, experienced by the ego as favorable or unfavorable, and finally analyzed and named by the intellect.

All of this activity is part of the seen; the activity of the three *gunas* is for the purpose of experience and emancipation. The question arises: emancipation for whom? This brings us to the point in meditation where

---

[94] See table, II-19.

we can separate the instrument of seeing from the seer. The faculty of discrimination is known as distinct from the observer.

~~~

I-46
tā eva sabījah samādhih
These engrossments are called *sabīj samādhi*, with seed.

Stages of *sabīj samādhi*	
savitarkā	Separate ego self from the gross body and physical world
nirvitarkā	Understand that happiness does not lie in physical objects
savicārā	Understand operation of mind with senses. Ego association with desire. Intellect's holding onto wrong notions.
nirvicārā	Ego relinquishes control to intellect. Modifications still.
ānanda	*Jivātman* dawns as seer.
asmitā	*Jivātman*, individual sense of self, established as seer.

The first four stages of *sabīj samādhi* provide the direct experience of the properties and functions of the elements and the faculties of knowing that interact with the elements. This inquiry promotes a more accurate understanding of our real identity. Through this process, the modifications of the *chitta* become still and the observer is reflected more clearly. Because the seed of *chitta*, now indicated as a mark or *lingam*, is adopting the seer, the medium appears as if existent, as if it is the seer. This is the experience of the *jivātman*, the individual soul or "I-amness."

The *chitta* or *lingam* is the seed of every individual being. No form exists without this seed form, and all faculties and experiences gained over lifetimes have migrated with it from unknown time. Because the seed is individual, we experience *ātman* as *jivātman*. The next two stages of development will occur at the level of *lingam*. First, "I-amness" is experienced, and then pure *chitta* is revealed and understood. All of this development is called *sabīj samādhi*, concentration with the seed.

These last two stages are a purification of the intellect. In *ānanda* and *asmitā samādhi*, we experience the individual form existing in relationship with *Īśvara*.

~~~

I-47
nirvicāra-vaiśāradye 'dhyātma-prasādah
In the perfection of *nirvicāra* there is complete lucidity of one's own self.

In *nirvicāra*, we have purged false concepts of our identity. The intellect is calm, quiet, and thoughtless. The first four stages of *samāpatti* or engrossment relate with objects, relationships and ideas external to the real self. As the seer becomes free from desire and attachment, the intellect becomes free of the impressions of objects, ideas and experiences. *Samādhi* is evenness of intellect.

Krishna explains, "To them, who are ever steadfast in practice, I give the Yoga of discrimination. Out of mere compassion for them, I become their *ātmabhava*, their inner sense of being, and by the brilliant lamp of knowledge, destroy the darkness born of ignorance."[95] Patañjali indicates this dawning as *adhyātma prasādah*. *Adhyātma* is knowledge of the soul and *prasādah* is grace. This is *ānanda samādhi*, when we realize the light of the real self. This realization is only possible once the external focus is eliminated. The intellect, free of pollution, is able to realize the seer as the source of existence and intelligence.

With the light of the real self, we experience unlimited happiness. This happiness is grace. It does not come from any other person, object, idea, or power. It is totally independent. It is very hard to go beyond *ānanda samādhi*. A *yogi* will live in this state for many lives because of the deep satisfaction gained through his or her effort. Again and again, a *yogi* may take birth, achieve this state, and enjoy the bliss of self, but this is not the end of practice, nor the aim of Yoga. The aim of devotional practice is to be one with *Īśvara*, to realize *jivātman* as the all-pervasive presence of *ātman*.

Individuation, no matter how satisfying, is not ultimate truth. We must be alert and continue to analyze and search for the cause of individuation. This process is undertaken in the light of wisdom. We realize that I-amness is coming from *ātman*, and *chitta* is only the medium of that expression. Nature and soul together manifest as *jivātman*. When we realize our position as the enlightener, separate from the medium, we become established in pure knowledge. We realize that the *chitta* is an instrument of experience, and individuation exists because of this medium. As we see our

---

[95] *Bhagavd Gita* X.10&11.

face in a mirror, *Īśvara* reflects in a pure *chitta* as the seer. When we are established in this realization, we experience *asmitā samādhi*.

~~~

I-48
rtambharā tatra prajñā
There comes wisdom that sees the truth.

In the thoughtless state, our *chitta* is free from desire, temptation, and fear. The intellect is stable and pure. The seer, the abode of knowledge, is realized and experienced. One of the properties of a pure intellect is the wisdom that sees truth and reflects reality. This becomes the means for final discrimination between the medium of nature and *ātman*.

With a pure intellect, we realize that *chitta* and *ātman* are separate, and that *jivātman* is only the presence of one undivided universal soul emanating from *Īśvara*.

~~~

I-49
śrutānumāna-prajñābhyām anyavisayā viśesārthatvāt
This wisdom is different from knowledge that is inferred or testimony that is heard because it has its own special distinctive object.

Realization is the direct experience of *Īśvara*, pure, eternal intelligence, existence and bliss, manifesting in the medium as the knower. When the intellect is free from attachment to the gross and subtle objects, we experience clarity. We have wisdom, and we see and know truth directly.

Wisdom is different from the knowledge gained through listening and inference. Inferred knowledge is based on indirect experience. Testimony is limited by the impossibility of describing realization with words. When the intellect has a direct experience, without the influences of emotion and desire, pure knowledge is fully fathomed. This wisdom ends our attachment to anything external. The distinction between the qualities of the seen and those of the self is realized.

~~~

I-50
taj-jah samskāro 'nya-samskāra-pratibandhī
The impression produced from this wisdom checks the impressions from previous disturbances.

When we realize that the self is separate from and above nature, including the medium of *chitta*, we free our self from the individual quality cast by the medium. The experience checks all previous impressions that happiness can be gained in any other way.

Krishna explains, "When a disciplined intellect rests in the self alone, free from longing for any object, then a practitioner is said to be established in Yoga. When the *chitta* comes to rest with the mind restrained by the practice of Yoga, and one beholds *ātman* as the self, one becomes content in the self alone. That infinite happiness can be grasped by a pure intellect. There is no greater gain than this. Being established in that position, one does not deviate from this reality."[96]

Humankind encourages misidentification. Society values accumulation and accomplishment. Because society values objects, we chase and hoard objects. We ascribe the qualities of the objects of the senses to the self. With a pure intellect, the qualities of the self are experienced independently. Our inner demand for existence and happiness is fulfilled by the experience of *Īśvara* dwelling within us as self. When we experience eternal happiness as the property of the self, we purge our impressions of previous and future disturbances.

~~~

I-51
tasyāpi nirodhe sarva-nirodhān nirbījah samādhih
Upon stoppage of even this truth-knowing wisdom, seedless *samādhi* comes, due to elimination of all impressions.

Nirbīj samādhi is not an intellectual or logical stage. It is not an objective experience, not a state that is seen and reached by discrimination. It is an experience above all the faculties of the seen, including *chitta*. So, for this reason Patañjali states there is a stoppage of even the truth-knowing wisdom. *Nirbīj samādhi* is a profound experience of oneness, a unity experienced as an immeasurable feeling of love that eliminates any

---

[96] *Bhagavd Gītā* VI.18, 20 & 22.

impression of separation. Any shred of doubt regarding a supreme existence and of separation from that is eliminated.

The *Brhadāranyaka Upanishad* provides a story regarding a bit of salt wanting to fathom the ocean, but when the salt jumps into the ocean, it dissolves into the ocean. A bit of salt cannot fathom the ocean because it has lost its own identity. In the same way, in *nirbīj samādhi* our sense of existence loses its individuality.[97]

The *Īsa Upanishad* highlights how this is an experience of grace beyond our discriminative attainment. The seer Dirghatamas reaches a point of realization where he sees how powerless he is to remove the seed of individuality and prays, "The face of truth is hidden with a golden orb (*chitta*). O Lord, who nourishes the world, please for my sake, I who am desirous and devoted to know the truth, please remove that covering so that I may see the truth." He has applied much effort and been devoted to seeking truth but finds that the experience is beyond the intellect. "O, Supreme *Purusha*, the form of knowledge itself, please collect your rays and gather your radiant light so I may behold your divine form." He then experiences, "That I am"—a state of unity with the supreme.[98]

Nirbīj samādhi is seedless because the seed, which has been necessary to provide an immanent, personal experience of the supreme, is transcended. We become one with the supreme realizing it is both immanent and transcendent. The seed of individuation becomes like a burned seed that will no longer sprout. In this devotional section of Yoga this supreme is called *Īśvara*.

~~~

---

[97] *Brhadāranyaka Upanishad* II.4.12.
[98] *Īsa Upanishad* 15&16.

Section II—*Sādhana Pada*

Practice

II-1

tapah-svādhyāyeśvara-pranidhānāni kriyā-yogah
Tapah (austerity), svādhyāya (self-study), and
Īśvara pranidhānā (surrender to the source of self),
make up the practice of kriyā yoga.

Kriyā means action. *Kriyā yoga* integrates practice and detachment with devotion. Together they form the action needed to still the modifications of *chitta* and realize the seer. This practice combines austerity, *tapah*, self-study, *svādhyāya*, and surrender to the source, *Īśvara pranidhānā*. We control and restrain our senses, mind and emotions with austerity; use the intellect in self-study; and align the ego and feelings with our divine source.

Austerity relates with physical, sensual, and mental awareness. Most of our suffering is caused by desires that arise in our minds and are satisfied through our senses. Because these desires cannot be satiated for more than a moment, we experience a lot of suffering with only momentary happiness. It is impossible to find lasting fulfillment through sensual experiences.

Desire is stimulated by the stored impressions of previous experience, called *samskāras*. These impressions in the *chitta* motivate us to act. Krishna tells Arjuna, "The knowledge of even the wise ones is obscured by this eternal enemy called desire. It is as all-consuming and insatiable as a fire."[99] If we do not moderate our senses, we are controlled and consumed by incessant desires. With discipline, *tapah*, we develop detachment, which pacifies the mind and restrains the senses.

Moderating the senses and controlling the mind is not easy. It is a challenge because the mind habitually wanders and leaps about. We tame the mind as we might tame a wild animal, lovingly and without force. The first step is to quietly observe the mind's tendencies and patterns. This observation helps us calm our senses. Next, we realize that the senses do not act alone, but are the instruments of the mind and the intellect. If we

---

[99] *Bhagavad Gītā* III.39.

tame the mind, training it to seek happiness by turning repeatedly toward its source, the mind gradually learns to trust and obey.

We are infatuated with the external world because we lack a rich inner life. The mind, without any ill intent, sabotages our efforts to turn inward because it is so easily attached. Once we turn the mind, it becomes eager to experience divinity. As we teach and guide the mind, we develop new habits. Gradually the mind becomes internally focused and the senses come under our control.

Austerity is the resistance we experience as we work to change our lives. *Tapah* translates as heat. We feel friction as we shift our habits from indulgence to temperance. Restraining the impulses of the senses often causes discomfort. When we are determined to make fundamental changes in our lives, we learn to tolerate this experience, even when it feels intolerable. As we observe our patterns and commit to change, there may be circumstances in our lives that are difficult to witness. We may realize that we are in situations or relationships that are unhealthy. Or, we may be in circumstances that we cannot change but that steadily challenge our spiritual path. The development of tolerance tempers us.

The practice of austerity includes postures, breathing exercises, and a pure diet. These support a *sattvic*, light-filled life, and they provide the strength, energy, and stamina to control our minds and senses. With all of these efforts, the mind gradually becomes calm and content. A quiet mind is necessary for enlightening self-study.

Svādhyāya, self-study, includes meditation with *mantra*, the study of scriptures, and introspection. When we chant a *mantra*, we create an inner vibration of sound that enlivens an experience of the seer. Scriptures support self-study by teaching the distinction between the self and non-self. Self-study stands on a foundation of knowledge established by those who have realized the self. The ideas and experiences of great seers help us find our way. This knowledge is a lighthouse, offering guidance and illumination for our path.

Seers are realized souls. Their knowledge and research into this experience of self is available to us. These guides have created maps. They outline routes and set out milestones along the way, assisting and directing us on the path. For *yoga* practitioners, there is no greater guidebook than the *Yoga Sūtras*. This compilation contains the gist of ancient knowledge from the Vedas and provides practical methods for realizing ultimate truth. We do not have to memorize all of the scriptures. As we become comfortable and fluent with a select few, the depth of this vast knowledge opens up to us. With practice and realization, we expand our comprehension. Using the guidance available to us, we avoid confusion.

Self-study helps us to understand our real self independent of circumstances. When our exploration of the self is supported by knowledge, we can establish a meaningful practice. As we explore our existence, our self-study yields to surrender. Each of us is familiar with a sense that "I am" and a feeling that "I exist." We can search within ourselves for the source of this awareness. Is it only related with our body? Western science is searching for the root of consciousness in the brain. Yoga establishes consciousness as distinct from nature. It is not to be found in any material substance. Consciousness and existence belong with the seer, and not with the seen or nature.

Great seers realized the source of consciousness and existence through meditation. When we meditate while chanting *mantra* the vibration calls us to the place where consciousness manifests in our *chitta*. In this place, we gradually realize the truth of our source. Knowledge combined with experience gives rise to the wisdom that shifts our identity away from the instruments of nature. With this shift, we accept and surrender to the source of life, *Īśvara*. This is *Īśvara pranidhāna*.

We are able to realize the source of life because it is not far from us; it is most near and dear to us. Practice leads us to experience that our sense of existence is contiguous with a larger existence and our consciousness emanates from this source. We do not find *Īśvara* through faith, but with knowledge, pure wisdom and direct experience. Patañjali tells us that *Īśvara* is a special kind of manifestation, untouched by misery, action, reaction, and accumulated impressions.[100] *Īśvara* is beyond suffering and actions.

As every ray of sunlight comes from the sun and cannot exist separate from the sun; we are one with our source and cannot exist separate from our source. When we realize our cause, we experience complete oneness and realize we are part and parcel of one integrated whole.

Kriyā yoga is a method for everyone. It is not a matter of faith. We use logic to understand the source of the self. With self-realization, our intellect becomes stable, calm, peaceful, and serene. A stable intellect is the pure abode of wisdom, the dwelling place for our knowledge and our experience of ultimate truth. Ignorance and misidentification create pain

---

[100] *Yoga Sūtras* I-24.

and suffering in our lives, and are the source of the *kleśas*, misery. Clear discernment of the truth removes our ignorance and misidentification.

~~~

II-2
samādhi-bhāvanārthah kleśa-tanū-karanārthaś ca
Kriyā yoga serves the purpose of realizing *samādhi* and attenuating the *kleśas,* the causes of pain.

Kriyā Yoga attenuates the *kleśas*, weakening them so they no longer perpetuate our suffering. The *kleśas* are layers of misunderstanding and ignorance that result from our identification with the world. The purpose of practice is to achieve *samādhi*, an even intellect. Merely reading and talking about practice will not help. As Saint Tulsidas tells us, if we are starving, only eating will help. Learning and talking about spirituality, without personal practice, cannot set us free.

We can think of suffering the way we consider disease. Treating a symptom is often an ineffective method for healing, whereas knowledge of the cause of a disease leads to successful treatment. Diseases are caused by lack or excess. Treatments include either the reduction of something excessive or the provision for deficiency. Until we look within, we suffer from excessive external attachments and a deficient awareness of our source.

Kriyā yoga reduces the excess activity in the mind through austerity and self-study. We diminish disturbances through the control of our senses, and we understand that our desires are triggered by our feelings of separation or egoism. We heal our unease by removing our ignorance. As our ignorance dissipates, we cure our deficient sense of self by seeking a direct experience of our self. As we realize who we really are, we surrender to our source. This is *samādhi*, which forever annihilates the cause of our suffering.

~~~

II-3
avidyāsmitā-rāga-dvesābhiniveśāh kleśāh
The causes of misery are ignorance, egoism, attachment, aversion, and the fear of death.

Ignorance, egoism, attraction, aversion, and the fear of death are the five afflictions.[101] *Avidyā* is the lack of real knowledge, and all other miseries spring from our ignorance. *Vidyā* is to see or to know. The Sanskrit prefix "*a*" means away from and so *avidyā* is the opposite of seeing and knowing. It afflicts the intellect and its first symptom is egoism. With egoism, we are ruled by attraction and aversion, and we have the compelling desire to control our lives and our world. Our greatest aversion is the fear of death, which is associated with all feelings of loss.

The binding effects of our ignorance manifest as *kleśas*, cause us suffering, and drive us to seek relief through behaviors that only deepen our misery. The results of our actions are called *karma*. *Karma* ties us to the world of cause and effect, birth and death, and the fluctuations of our suffering. Patañjali will soon follow these *sutras* on the *kleśas* with the theory of *karma*.

~~~

II-4
avidyā ksetram uttaresām prasupta-tanu-vicchinnodārānām
Ignorance causes the other four miseries, whether they are dormant, attenuated, interrupted, or active.

Avidyā, a lack of knowledge about the reality of our existence, causes the other four miseries. *Avidyā* is our fundamental affliction, and all other miseries are its symptoms. Egoism is our impressions projected as pride, desire, anger, passion, lust, and greed. It produces cravings and aversions, *raga* and *dvesa*. Our struggle with attachments and aversions gives rise to *abhiniveśa*, the fear that those things that we cling to will come to an end. All suffering is ultimately related with fear. Once we accept the limited form of the ego as our real self, we are caught in the cycle of desires and aversions. We are afraid that we will not get what we want, and we fear we will have to endure what we do not want. Ultimately, we fear loss, we fear separation, and we fear death. Fear is the virulent aspect of all our suffering, and like all the miseries, fear is rooted in our ignorance.

We carry our impressions of wrong thinking, but they do not express all at once; they may be dormant, in a state of attenuation, interrupted, or active. Their power over us depends on how much we have invested in them. Every day, we see evidence that nothing in this world is permanent;

---

[101] See also *Tattva Samāsa* 12.

even our desires are constantly changing. What we craved yesterday no longer satisfies us today. We look for the newest version or the better model. We tire of our friends; we get bored with our partner and the job that once thrilled us. New temptations continually arise to fuel our feelings of desire.

Spending our lives focused on status and pleasure, and living in denial that our bodies will die, encourages egoism. Egoism makes us more heavily invested in attachments, aversions and the fear of death. We become susceptible to comparison, jealousy, dishonesty and greed. As we rush toward accumulation in one form or another and run away from the things we hate and fear, it is difficult to see the path within that leads to peace and tranquility. Though we are faced with the truth that we can never be satisfied by our fluctuating desires in a changing world, our ignorance compels us to try anyway.

Krishna tells us, "Dwelling on an enjoyable object breeds attachment and creates the seed of desire. If the desire is fulfilled, greed appears; if thwarted, anger appears. Anger brings delusion and destroys memory. When a person loses memory, the intellect becomes weak and the mind has more powerful attachments to the senses. From deep attachment to worldly objects, a person ruins his life."[102] Like a person playing in the surf who gets tumbled by a giant wave, we become disoriented. We must re-orient ourselves and align with the truth of our existence so that we may find lasting peace and happiness. As we learn to act with restraint, we interrupt the flow of desires and attenuate the impulses of the *kleśas*. This subdues our desires and quiets the *kleśas*, eventually ending their production.

~~~

II-5
anityāśuci-duhkhānātmasu nitya-śuci-suckhātma-khyātir avidyā
Ignorance is accepting the finite, impure, suffering-inducing non-self as the eternal, pure, blissful real self.

When we believe the body is the true self and we credit the properties of the body to the seer, we are ignorant of our real self. Our true self is unknown to us because of our misidentification.

---

102 *Bhagavad Gita* II.62&63.

Chitta is the medium of nature required for the properties of the seer to manifest. If the seer were electricity, the *chitta* would be the filament encased in a light bulb. Like electricity, the seer is all pervasive and unseen; and like a light bulb, the *chitta* is only illuminated when it receives its animating power.

The intellect, ego, and mind arise from the causal body of *chitta*.[103] The causal body is the seed of the subtle body, and the subtle body is the seed of the gross body. We emerge into existence in these three stages, but when we identify with the causal, subtle or physical body, instead of with our inspiring source, we suffer. This is *avidyā*, mistaking the finite, impure cause of suffering as the permanent, pure source of happiness.

All three bodies—causal, subtle and gross—are projections of nature, and nature is constantly changing. Change is an intrinsic quality of nature. Our physical bodies are most certainly mortal. Death is the destination of the body—this is an unavoidable truth. As Krishna simply states, "He who is born will one day die; the body is neither eternal nor permanent."[104] Impurities are also an undeniable aspect of the physical body. In this world of tumultuous change and entropy, there is no perfection. Likewise, misery is related with physical existence. All of the situations that cause us suffering—our confusion, attachments, and fears—are related with our lives as human beings.

There are people with so much pride in their own form that they feel superior to others. Racism and other types of prejudice spring from ignorance. No physical markers identify a person as worthy or worthless. Everyone is a manifestation of the same inspiring source enlivening the world of nature. If we are ignorant of this, it is easy to dehumanize groups of people who are different from us, and when we do this we cause tremendous suffering.

The body is made up of the five primordial elements.[105] We may appear to be different, but we all exist because the same building blocks of life have come together in our bodies. We survive by breathing the same air and sharing space on the same planet. In our ignorance, we may believe we are superior to others and that others do not have the same rights to

---

[103] See also *Tattva Samāsa* 17.

[104] *Bhagavad Gita* II.27.

[105] The five primordial elements are called the *bhūtas*: earth, water, fire, air, and space. They are the most *tamasic* expression of *prakriti*, unmanifest energy.

the world's resources. Again and again, ignorance causes devastating misery.

In the *Mahabharata*, King Yudhishthira is asked about the greatest wonder in the world. He answers, "The greatest wonder is that, although we see people dying daily, those who are alive think they will never die." When we realize that the body is separate from the self, we have *vidya*, knowledge. With proper knowledge, we free ourselves from bondage and suffering.

~~~

II-6
drg-darsana-saktyor ekatmatevasmita
Egoism is identification of the seer with the seeing power.

As mentioned, *chitta* is the abode of our beliefs called impressions. These impressions form our ability to discriminate and make judgments, the function of the intellect. Patañjali indicates that the intellect is the seeing power, and explains that when the seer is blended with this instrument an egoistic self called *asmita* is produced.[106] The two distinct powers of the seer and the intellect are blended into one individual identity.

Misunderstanding first occurs when the individual medium of *chitta* becomes animated as it adopts the qualities of the all-pervasive seer—existence and consciousness. This individual quality of the medium produces a sense of I, which combined with the qualities of existence and consciousness is experienced as I-exist or I-am. The inert medium appears as if existent and conscious and is mistaken as the source of our life.

The shadow of I-exist produces an experience of separation, which yields a sense of lack, thus initiating an inner demand for wholeness. Externalizing this inner demand for wholeness, we turn outward through the senses toward the world of objects as a way of fulfilling it. We form many beliefs while interpreting and defining the value of the world around us, which develops our discriminating function, the intellect. In this process the initial stage of I-am, *asmi*, is cognitively blended with the impressions of the intellect forming an egoistic self called *asmita*—*I am this* or *I am that*. Egoism is the power of doing or attaining this or that.

Seers have compared us to silkworms. From within its own body, a silkworm creates fine thread and covers itself with this thread, building a

---

[106] *Yoga Sutras* II-6.

cocoon in which it dies. In the same way, from within ourselves, we create the thinking that *I am this* and *this is mine*. We surround ourselves with an accumulation of thoughts and things that cannot save us, and in this way we suffocate ourselves. When we search deeply, we realize that nothing belongs to us. The intellect, ego, mind, senses, body, and all objects around us are projections of nature. Nature evolves into everything in existence, from subtle to gross. Nature and spirit are both eternal and infinite. Nature provides the medium and spirit inspires the medium. We are all a manifestation of consciousness in nature, but we have lost our wholeness.

~~~

II-7 and 8
sukhānuśayī rāgah
Attachment is holding on to prior happiness.

duhkhānuśayī dvesah
Aversion is holding on to prior pain.

When our sense of I-am appears, believing its entity is separate from the source, then we accept diversity as the ultimate truth. Everything we enjoy fosters desire and everything we fear generates aversion. We use the word love when we speak of our attachments, but the emotion we feel is not love—it is infatuation we desire. Real love is desireless, and it is related with infinite wisdom and bliss. Love is experienced when we give and receive without desire. The world of give and take, lust and satisfaction, greed and accumulation, is the realm of desire and hate.

Desire and revulsion cause suffering. *Rāga* is attraction, temptation, and passion. *Dvesa* is aversion, repulsion, and resentment. Once we identify with someone or something, we fear losing that dear person or thing. When we lose a precious relationship or object, we feel rage and misery. The fear of loss is one of the ways our attachments cause our suffering.

Identification and attachment breed cravings for enjoyment. When we desire the objects of the senses, we seek to attain what we want. If we are satisfied, we feel pleased and our attachment grows. When we are thwarted, aversion grows and we feel anger and frustration. Our attachments build and fortify our attractions and aversions, which obstruct our practice. They are like kidnappers, stealing us away from the seer.

~~~

II-9

sva-rasa-vāhī viduso'pi tathārūdho 'bhiniveśah
**The firmly established inborn fear of separation from the
body, even in the wise, is the misery of fearing death.**

Ultimately our outward focus leads us to identification with the body
as self. *Abhiniveśa* is rooted in our will to survive. The survival instinct is
natural—we are born with it. We have experienced birth and death many
times, and the impressions or *samskāras* of death reside in our *chitta*. This
creates an inner anxiety related to death and separation. We do not want to
carry the impressions of mortal fear, but they come with us from one life
to another. Patañjali states that this fear causes suffering even in the
learned and wise.

Our fear of losing things, relationships and status is also *abhiniveśa*. We
do not want to be fearful, yet our attempts to ease our fears only increase
them. In the Cold War, the United States and the Soviet Union were
locked in an arms race with the goal of security, but each more powerful
weapon triggered more fear. The ever-present realities of life—old age,
sickness, and death—spur fears that lead us to spiritual inquiry.

~~~

II-10

te pratiprasava-heyāh sūksmāh
**The root causes of pain, in their subtle form,
are to be ended by inverse propagation.**

Heya refers to what ought to be removed, that is, the *kleśas*. *Pratiprasava*
means to go in the reverse direction, or to merge the effect into its cause.
The *kleśas* are the five causes of suffering that reside in the *chitta* in subtle
form. Wrong knowledge is the primary cause, initiating egoism, attachment,
aversion, and fear. Practice enables us to merge the effects into their cause,
ending suffering.

The theory of causation underlies the principles of Sāmkhya and Yoga.
Because every effect has a cause, we remove the effect of suffering by
seeking and removing its cause. If the cause remains unchanged, the effect
cannot be annihilated. Yoga's methods help us collect our senses from
their objects and merge them back into the mind. Since the mind is the
expression of ego, we merge the mind back into ego and then we merge
the ego back into its source in the intellect. From the intellect, we seek the
source of self. Dwelling on the source of our intelligence and existence

leads us to the seer. In that state we achieve peace, and our suffering is annihilated. Our ignorance of the real self causes our suffering.

The *kleśas* have three states: small and weak, *tanu*; stronger and scattered, *vichchinna*; and strongest and manifest, *udar*. The *kleśas* are not destroyed until their cause is terminated. They arise with the emergence of our feelings of individuation and separation in the *chitta* and are the result of *avidyā*, wrong knowledge. Only when we understand and realize the true qualities of the self can individuation and separation cease. As long as *avidyā* exists, the fluctuations of pleasure and pain will be experienced. In order to end suffering, we must realize that it is not possible to satisfy the demand for bliss with external means.

As we minimize the power of the *kleśas*, we must remain vigilant. They may become less obvious, but they remain with us as dormant impressions in the intellect. They lurk in an attenuated form until we become established in the seer. Any time the *kleśas* find a chance to spring out they quickly overpower and scatter our energy. If we are not watchful, any vulnerable situation shatters our stability. Without steady vigilance, any one of the *kleśas* can ensnare us and drag us back towards suffering.

Through practice, we realize that our individual consciousness is part and parcel of pure consciousness, and the real self is beyond limitation. Consciousness is not a partial thing, and whatever is non-component is infinite, limitless, and beyond all obstacles and barriers. The seer is a manifestation of an all-pervasive conscious existence. When we realize our self, we know we are not the limited body. We are the seer, and we gain experience and emancipation using the body as an instrument. In this state of realization, we are free of delusion and infatuation, and our wisdom is established and stable. All suffering ends when ignorance, *avidyā*, no longer activates effects in the *kleśas*.

~~~

II-11
dhyāna-heyās tad-vrttayah
By meditation the five causes of suffering are annihilated.

Meditation is the method that makes the *chitta* modeless, without impulse. In meditation, we quiet our activity and seek the state of awareness where we see the impulses that motivate our actions. This practice gives us the chance to move above the mind and its cravings. Although we are willing to strive for many things, we resist setting aside time for meditation. The practice of sitting in a calm and quiet state, even for a few minutes, is daunting. We do the most ridiculous things to distract ourselves but find it almost impossible to be quiet for a brief time. Most of us feel skittish as we begin meditation practice, sometimes even terrified, about observing our thoughts. But gradually, turning within brings solace and we lose our resistance.

Krishna teaches us to establish a state that is quiet, without fear, and fixed in *brahmacharya*. In this state, our minds and emotions are controlled. With our thoughts fixed on our source, we sit in concentration and devotion. [107] Meditation brings us into the present moment. This is challenging. Most of the time, we are speculate about the future or ruminate on the past. Our habitual mental state dwells in the past and the future, and we are rarely present. This is unfortunate because it is only in the present moment that we are free from doubt and fear.

In meditation, the activity of the *chitta* settles and our awareness shifts from thinking to I-amness. I-amness is above the mind and is the gateway to pure intelligence, existence and bliss. First we seek an untainted experience of I-am. In this state, the intellect helps us realize our relationship with pure consciousness. *Brahmacharya* is the control of our emotions and desires. With this restraint we are able to turn our attention toward the seer. The seer is not found in the past or the future. It is omnipresent and must be found in the present moment. There is no division of time or space in consciousness. When misidentification of the self with the modes of the *chitta* is removed, the intellect relinquishes past and future and we experience the I-am as the seer, part and parcel of an all-pervasive consciousness. In the light of this experience, the *kleśas* lose their power.

Through meditation, we gradually reach the thoughtless, modeless state of the *chitta*. In this state, the reflection of the seer is steadily perceived and we clearly distinguish between the qualities of nature, and the qualities of consciousness. At this stage of discrimination and self-illumination, the identification of seer with the modes of *chitta* is eradicated. This is supreme detachment[108] and it is the end of all suffering.

~~~

---

[107] *Bhagavad Gītā* VI.14.
[108] *Yoga Sūtras* I-16.

II-12
kleśa-mūlah karmāśayo drstādrstā-janma-vedanīyah
The accumulations of *karma* are rooted in the *kleśas* and give their result either in the present or future.

Karma is the motive that drives our actions. Every action has three parts. The action itself is *kriyā*; the doer is *karta*; and the motive is *karma*. The result of an action depends on the motive behind the action. Different motives for the same action produce different results. For example, when a surgeon cuts a body to remove disease, the motive is to heal. But when a mugger cuts a body to get money, the motive is greed. The same action brings the surgeon respect and the mugger time in prison. Different motives yield different results.

The effects of our actions appear in two forms: *drista*, visible, and *adrista*, invisible. The fruits of our actions may come in our present life or in the future. Our reservoir of *karma* is the cause of our birth, death, and the cycle of our suffering. Our current life is the result of our *karma* from past motivations, and our next life will be structured according to our present motives. Our existing bodies and circumstances arise from the intentions of our previous actions. When desire motivates our actions, our actions bring us suffering. Krishna states, "Greed, activity, the undertaking of actions, unrest, and longing arise when *rajas* is predominant."[109] Actions motivated by selfish passion perpetuate misery.

We do not like owning responsibility for our situation. There is a story of a pigeon that could not fly. When he saw a cat coming, he closed his eyes in an effort to escape his fate. This is our human nature—we close our eyes and think that death will not see us. We hope that the results of our manipulations and untoward actions will not be discovered and will not find us, but the results of our actions inevitably come home. Among thousands of cows, a little calf searches and finds its own mother. Among billions of people in the world, the results of our actions return to us. We reap as we sow. The fruit of uplifting *karma* is happiness and the fruit of destructive *karma* is suffering. Human life swings between moments of happiness and tremendous suffering.

~~~

---

[109] *Bhagavad Gītā* XIV.12.

II-13
sati mūle tad-vipāko jātyāyur-bhogāh
As long as the *kleśas* are at the root, the *karmas* ripen into three fruits: the form or species of life, the span of life, and the circumstances of life

Every human life is a continuation. Our souls have gathered the impressions of many previous births. We have lived as insects, reptiles, birds, and mammals, and in each life we performed action. Our actions in non-human species followed natural instincts and were outside the laws of *karma*. In human life, our actions are motivated by desire. How many times we have lived as humans, we do not know. But in each human lifetime, we contributed to a reservoir of *karma* with countless actions. When our *karma* ripens, this reservoir flows into our birth, species, span of life, and experience. We each have unique *karma*. Our particular characteristics are a manifestation of our *karma*.

Action itself does not cause bondage. We are bound by our motives and desires. Nature is insentient. It does not have motives. Insentient nature cannot bind sentient beings. It is our attachment to the limited body that causes our feelings of separation and emptiness, leading us to identify with the material world and embed our fear of loss. With our desire to grab and hoard, we are setting traps for ourselves. As long as we have wrong thinking, our actions bind us down to their results. The results manifest in our birth, *jāti*; span of life, *āyuh*; and circumstances, *bhoga*.

Our fundamental inability to discriminate between the qualities of the seer and the objects of perception causes attachment and pain. Delusion and infatuation with external experience cause suffering, but it is possible to work with objects and relate to people without generating misery. When we are free of desire, we can act in the world while motivated to serve. All of our actions become an offering to the source of our lives.

Our prior actions have led us to this moment in which we are free to choose how we will go forward. We cannot blame *karma*, time, or God for our current circumstances. We have brought ourselves to our present situation and we are free to use or misuse this life. If we continue to chase pleasure, we misuse the gift of human life. If we spend our lives and resources for upliftment, we move toward freedom. The laws of *karma* operate in human life, and it is within human life that we free ourselves.

Saint Tulsidas' parents died a few days after he was born. The maidservant who cared for him also died when he was four. After her death, village children fed him until, one year later, a great saint took him in. This abandoned boy gradually became a great seer who inspired many people to live a divine life. A lack of parenting is used as an excuse for all kinds of behavior. We must remember that our *karma* creates our circumstances and we choose how to move forward. Our current situation is the result of our previous *karma*, and our current efforts determine where we go from here.

If we believe in fate, we do not think our efforts can overcome our fate, and we continue along in accordance with our impressions. We have free will. We can direct our efforts to free ourselves from our impressions, and from the cycle of birth, suffering and death. Our great teachers direct us to exercise our free will and strive for the emancipation of the soul.

~~~

II-14
te hlāda-paritāpa-phalāh punyāpunya hetutvāt
Those results give happiness or suffering according to their cause being virtuous or non-virtuous.

Every action results in enjoyment or suffering. Helpful actions bring enjoyment and harmful actions draw suffering. Even our enjoyment ends in suffering because the source of our enjoyment inevitably changes or passes away. We cannot change the results of our actions. But we can observe our actions and analyze our motives and abilities.

There are four types of action: *karma, sukarma, satkarma* and *vikarma*. *Karma* is the duty related with our abilities and our position within our family, community and country. We all have responsibilities and obligations within our circumstances. A functioning society depends on the contributions of each member.

Sukarma is virtuous work motivated by the desire to achieve heaven, while *satkarma* is action inspired by the inner demand of emancipation. *Satkarma* frees us from the cycle of birth and death. Finally, *vikarma* is wrong action, which should be avoided. Destructive actions carry us away from truth and cause great suffering.

We should not confuse *satkarma* with *sukarma*. *Satkarma* is our effort to attain emancipation, while *sukarma* is virtuous work and religious activity driven by the desire for heavenly pleasure or earthly rewards. Whether we are taking care of our responsibilities or performing religious work, we must free our actions from desire. The work of *satkarma* is free from the judgment of virtuous or non-virtuous. Detached from virtue and vice, it leads us to the abode of eternal bliss.

The methods of Yoga teach *satkarma*. Our efforts purify our intellects, minds, and hearts, enabling us to realize the self as one with its source. In the *Bhagavad Gītā*, this is called *karma yoga*. We do not chase after the mind's cravings and get lost in a thicket of worldly pleasures. Our actions and efforts are inspired by our inner demand for wholeness.

~~~

II-15
parināma tāpa-sanskāra-duhkhair guna-vrtti-virodhāc
ca duhkham eva sarvam vivekinah
According to wise people, worldly objects cause suffering because: enjoyment will one day end; others will have more than you; you hold onto the memory of previous experience; and the differing natures of the *gunas* are contradictory.

Even if we find enjoyment through external means, our enjoyment always leads to suffering. As nature inevitably changes, we lose what we enjoy or we lose our ability to enjoy. Someone always has more than we do, and comparisons lead to suffering. We cannot enjoy life when we are stuck ruminating about past pleasure. And we suffer from the fluctuations of the *gunas*, which never exist in a balanced state. Even when our search for pleasure yields success, we are making a bed of misery for ourselves.

Krishna advises, "The acts of sacrifice, gifts and austerities should not be relinquished. They should be performed. But these acts should be done without motive, relinquishing attachment and the fruits thereof."[110] The result of good works is happiness. But eternal happiness only comes with realization and emancipation, not from virtuous activities. Virtuous works performed with even the slightest selfish motive generate three kinds of pain: *parināma*, *tāpa*, and *samskāra*.

When our action, even virtuous action, is motivated by the desire for a certain outcome, it leads to suffering because the reward is finite. When we work hard, earn money, and open a savings account, we can enjoy spending the money from our previous effort. When that money is used up, our ability to enjoy our savings ends and our insecurity resumes.

Parināma duhk is the pain that arises when the fruit from previous actions expires. We enjoy the fruit until these benefits come to an end,

---

[110] *Bhagavad Gītā* XVIII.5&6.

leaving us cut off and anxious. Our souls feel bereft. The result of virtuous work is heavenly enjoyment. In heaven, we enjoy the results of our previous actions, but we cannot perform worthy actions. When the results of virtue end, we take birth again. This pain is like that of a rich person who is suddenly poor. *Parināma duhk* is the pain that comes after the fruit of virtuous work expires.

Tāpa duhk is jealousy. Envious comparisons are established in egoism. Even in heaven we have *asmita*, a sense of individuality. Jealousy exists in heaven, as we observe others enjoying more. Any time we are jealous of another's happiness, we feel pain. Comparisons breed egoism when we have more and frustration when we have less.

We suffer *samskāra* pain as we recall past enjoyment. Our memory traces past experiences over and over again. The pain associated with memory is *samskāra duhk*.

All actions motivated by desire lead to pain. Even if we find some happiness, our happiness ends and we suffer. All pleasure ends with the pain of loss. Our pain is relieved by pleasure. Pleasure ends in pain, and pain ends in pleasure. This cycle continues endlessly until we free ourselves from desire and end our identification and attachment.

Wise people know that even virtue leads to pain. The source of pain lies in the three *gunas*, which are at odds with each other. *Sattoguna* gives light and inspires virtue, *rajoguna* creates movement and passion, and *tamoguna* brings stability and inertia. One of these states dominates the *chitta*, bringing its own result. The dominance of one overpowers the presence of the others. When we are dominated by the desires of *rajoguna*, the insight of *sattva* is ignored, and the need for the rest of *tamoguna* is pushed aside. The driving passion of *rajas* and the heavy darkness of *tamas* clearly bring pain. But even the virtue inspired by *sattoguna* leads to pain because there is no state of nature that can provide lasting, blissful peace.

~~~

II-16
heyam duhkham anāgatam
The pain that has not yet come is to be avoided.

We are responsible for our actions and their results. Our previous actions have brought us to our current circumstances. As our present situation is the result of our past actions, what we do now creates our future. If we are currently in a challenging or discouraging situation, we should not be afraid. We must become aware in the present moment, avoiding the mistakes that brought us our current suffering. Otherwise, our future will be a continuation of our current difficulties.

We should not bring our past pain into the present; it cannot harm us. And we cannot change the present moment; it is already with us. But the pain that is yet to come originates in our current actions. We can prevent future pain by working with our motives in the present moment.

The teaching of *heya, heya hetu, hāna, hānopāya* tells us we can find freedom. *Heya* is what should be avoided: suffering. *Heya hetu* teaches the cause of pain that can be removed. *Hāna* assures us that suffering can be eliminated because pain is neither a property of the soul nor a property of nature. And *hānopāya* indicates there is a method available to us. These principles are discussed in the following *sūtras*.

~~~

II-17
drastr-drśyayoh sanyogo heya-hetuh
The cause of suffering is the identification of the seer with the seen.

The cause of suffering is *sanyoga*, the identification of the seer with the seen. Manifestation is the result of two distinct and separate powers: the seer, spirit; and the seen, nature. Like the light of electricity, the seer becomes known through a medium. Light shines in a light bulb; the seer manifests in the *chitta*. There are two causes that together make the light of the self: the material cause of the *chitta*, and the illuminating spirit. Suffering is not a quality of the seer or of nature. Suffering comes with the misunderstanding that arises when these two properties manifest.

When the seer manifests in *chitta*, the equilibrium of the three attributes of nature is disturbed. This movement causes the *chitta* to modify, awakening the intellect, ego, and mind. The individual soul is the illumination of spirit appearing in the form of the *chitta*. Many philosophers describe the soul as a child. Nature is the mother of the soul, and spirit is the father. "I" is a manifestation of spirit and "am" is a projection of nature. Nature is eternal, but its effects create individuality and diversity. When we do not realize that our I-am is a manifestation of spirit in a medium of nature, we are ignorant of the source of our life. In our ignorance, we do not honor our divine parents and we turn away from divine love.

125

When we encounter external objects and experiences, the I-am illuminates the experience. The senses collect the specific properties of the experience; the mind modifies, displaying these qualities as waves of thoughts and images; our ego reacts to the stimulation, choosing to appreciate or wishing to disregard the stimulation; and the intellect reflects and categorizes the experience. All of these are modifications of nature and are changeable. The seer only witnesses and observes. We choose to become identified with the activities of our body, senses and mind, ego and intellect. When our real self becomes identified with these levels of nature, we experience limitation, bondage, and suffering. Identification means to value something outside the self as a quality of the self.

By accepting our individual form and turning away from our source, we draw suffering into our lives. Yoga's methods help us remove our ignorance and realize the source of our existence. The modifications of *chitta* are instruments for gaining experience and emancipating the I-am.

~~~

II-18
prakāśa-kriyā-sthiti-śīlam bhūtendriyātmakam bhogāpavargārtham dryśam
The seen, which has three attributes of light, movement and stability, projects in the elements and senses, and is for experience and emancipation.

Nature, *prakriti*, has three attributes: light, movement and stability. The roots *pra*, *kr*, and *iti*, are found in the terms for the *gunas* used in this verse. *Sattoguna* is called *prakash*, luminous light. *Rajoguna* is *kriyā*, subtle movement. *Tamoguna* is *sthiti*, stability. The three *gunas* are *pra-kr-iti*, nature. The senses and the elements, which are the objects of the senses,[111] are projections of nature. Nature provides the means for the self to experience nature and to find freedom from bondage. This is the purpose of all activity: to achieve knowledge through experience.

The first mantra of the *Isa Upanishad* states that the Lord pervades all that exists. Enjoy pleasure, but do not become attached or greedy. Remain

---

[111] The *bhutas* are the five primordial elements of nature: earth, water, fire, air and space. The *indriyas* are the five cognitive senses: eyes, ears, nostrils, skin and tongue; and the five active senses: mouth, hands, feet, generative and excretive organs; and the mind.

cautious, because whose wealth is it?[112] The elements and objects of the senses are to be enjoyed with detachment through the senses and organs of action. All of these modifications are the three qualities of nature. Nature provides the material for experience, and, when used properly and without attachment, it provides the tools for emancipation.

Nature does not obstruct our path to emancipation. It is our misidentification of the self with nature that causes bondage. *Bhoga* is experience with a focus on the senses, but when we change our focus; our experiences bring knowledge, which is the property of the self. Often, we divide our lives into sacred and secular routines. We create boundaries and express our spirituality within certain buildings or rituals, separate from our daily work and relaxation. Life cannot be split in this manner. We must be conscious that every moment is divine. Everything we do leaves an impression in the *chitta*. If we constantly remember the source of life, all of our actions become service and everything that arises is perceived as a gift of grace.

We can feel one of two ways about the material world. The first is a feeling of ownership, and the second is a feeling of gratitude. When we feel possessive, we develop attachments and think that our glory lies in accumulation. When we feel gratitude we simply participate in nature appreciating that our needs can be met. When we accumulate, the means become the goal. When the motive is to acquire objects we lose connection with the whole.

The purpose of nature is to provide experience and emancipation. According to Yoga philosophy, everything is for us to use, not to possess. Nature cannot be owned. Nature changes in every moment, and our attempts to claim and hoard the objects of nature lead to our suffering. Nature provides for us and we should use what she offers with gratitude.

~~~

II-19
viśesāviśesa-lingamātrālingāni guna-parvāni
The states of the *gunas* are gross, subtle, causal and formless.

According to Sāmkhya, there are eight root causes, which further modify into sixteen modifications. The eight root causes are *prakriti*, the

---

[112] "All this, whatsover moves or is changeable, including that which moves not, is enveloped by the Lord. One should be disciplined and enjoy. Do not covet anybody's wealth, for whose wealth is this?"

intellect, ego and five subtle elements. The sixteen modifications are the mind, the five cognitive senses, the five active senses, and the five gross elements. The ego creates the mind, the five cognitive senses, and the five active senses. The *tanmātras*, subtle elements, originate from the ego and are the cause of the five gross elements.[113] The chart below summaries the states of energy related with the unfoldment of unmanifest nature into human form according to Sāmkhya.

Alingam	Unmanifest formless *prakriti*			
Lingam	*Chitta*—the causal mark or seed, the intellect			
Aviśesa	Subtle root causes			
	Ego	Five *Tanmātras*		
		Sound		
		Touch		
		Form		
		Taste		
		Smell		
Viśesa	16 modifications – the gross			
	Mind	Cognitive Senses	Active Senses	Elements
		Ears	Mouth	Space
		Skin	Hands	Air
		Eyes	Legs	Fire
		Tongue	Reproduction Organs	Water
		Nose	Organs of Elimination	Earth

---

113 See *Tattva Samāsa* 2 and 3.

Prakriti has three attributes: light, movement and stability, which cause nature to transform into effects and create forms. *Prakriti*, or nature, is the source of the manifested world. Nature is one whole, encompassing both the formless state and all projections into manifestation. The manifest, *vyakta*, is everything that is visible and perceptible. The unmanifest, *avyakta*, is the source of whatever is visible and perceptible. The *gunas* move from an imperceptible state into perceptible and visible forms. The three *gunas* exist at every level of nature's energy.

This verse opens with the two terms *viśesa* and *aviśesa*. Aviśesa is subtle. It is not visible, but is perceptible. The subtle elements, called *tanmātras*, sound, touch, form, taste and smell, are the cause of the five gross elements, which constitute the physical universe, including our human body. The gross state is visible, *viśesa*, and perceptible.

Lingam means mark or sign. *Lingam* is the individual seed or medium of objects and beings. In our human form, nature manifests as our causal, subtle, and physical bodies. When pure consciousness manifests in the causal medium of *chitta*, the intellect, the ego, the mind, the senses, and the elements gather around this seed. The process is similar to the growth of a tree. A tree lives in a seed in subtle form until it has the opportunity to sprout, growing branches, leaves and fruit. Accumulation makes this possible.

Accumulation occurs when many things are held together in one place. Emanation, the production of form, is the result of accumulation.[114] According to Sāmkhya, nature is the material cause of manifestation, whereby all phenomena emanate from the transformations and modifications of the three *gunas*. These three attributes modify into subtle elements, which produce the gross elements. Gross forms are combinations of the five gross elements of space, air, heat, water and earth.

The unmanifest state is referred to as *alinga* in this *sūtra*. *Alinga* is imperceptible, and can only be understood to exist by its effect—the phenomenal universe. This universe is a projection of nature. Unmanifest nature is beyond vision, beyond perception, beyond everything. One can only infer the existence of unmanifest nature by its projection into form.

Scientists declare that energy is the cause of the material word. Although scientists cannot explain what energy is, they are able to define it by what it is not. They describe energy as formless, weightless, colorless,

---

[114] *Tattva Samāsa* 17

and limitless. No scientist can show you energy. We can only know and study it by its effects. Unmanifest energy is beyond our vision and perception, and the first manifestation of energy is also beyond our vision and perception. With the naked eye we cannot see atoms, nor can we see the electrons, protons and neutrons of which atoms are made. With the naked eye we only see combinations of atoms.

~~~

II-20
drastā drśi-mātrah śuddho 'pi pratyayānupaśyah
The seer is pure consciousness. It is pure, even when observing the modes of *chitta*.

Here, following the explanation of the seen, the seer is now being defined. The seer and the seen come from one source, a Supreme Being that emerges as the living self along with all names and forms, called *Īśvara* in *sūtra* I-23. *Īśvara* is the manifested form of an unseen *Brahman*.

The Vedas and Upanishads hold the position that there is only one, imperishable, Supreme Self called *Brahman*. The word *Brahman* is derived from the root *brinh*, which means to expand. Just as a spider produces a web from within itself, and then dwells in its web; *Brahman* projects the universe from within itself, and then enters and resides in it. [115] The *Bhagavad Gītā* tells that *Brahman* pervades all and has the intrinsic quality to dwell within all individual beings as self. [116]

Brahman is both transcendent and immanent. It is one, imperceptible, unchanging living self, yet providing an immanent and personal experience of self within every individual being. This was discussed in I-23 as soul, *ātman*, and individual soul, *jivātman*.

The Vedas say that *Brahman* is beyond description. It is indicated as *satyam jñānam anantam*. [117] *Satyam* means eternal truth; *jñānam* means pure knowledge; *anantam* is infinity. The individual soul experiences *satyam* as existence, *jñānam* as intelligence, and *anantam* as bliss. Bliss is the experience of not being bound, limited or finite. In this state, our sense of self experiences an expansiveness—the bliss of *Brahman*.

The seer is independent of the seen and remains unmixed, even while observing the modifications of *chitta*. The seer is both transcendent and

---

[115] *Mundaka Upanishad* I.1.7.
[116] *Bhagavad Gītā* VIII.3.
[117] *Taittirīya Upanishad* II.1.2

immanent. It enlightens all *chittas* and yet it exists above and beyond all bodies because it is distinctly unmixed in the material world. As the sun brings light to all eyes, but lives above all eyes, one self enlightens all *chittas* and exists beyond all forms of nature.

The seer is the enlightener and observer of nature's movement. Although the seer appears to mingle, it remains pure and untainted by nature. The properties of the seer dwell in every living form. This gives the seer an appearance of plurality, but the seer remains one and cannot be divided. The Upanishads state: "The sun is the eye of all beings, yet it is not affected by the defects in other beings' eyes."[118] The seer is unaffected by the modifications of the *chitta*.

In itself, fire has no smell. Smell is not a property of fire, but a property of the fuel it burns. If we put incense in a fire, it creates a sweet fragrance. When leather burns, it smells foul. Just as we associate the attributes of the fuel to the fire, we ascribe the qualities of nature to the seer. When the *chitta* is purified, the real form of the seer is known. The aim of all spiritual practices is to purify the *chitta*.

~~~

II-21
tad-artha eva drśyasyātmā
Everything in existence (the seen) is for that (the seer).

Nature emanates and accumulates solely for the seer. Kapila states *anugrahaḥ sargaḥ*,[119] emanation is accumulation. Emanation, the projection of this universe, occurs by accumulation, the amassing of elements. Spirit attracts the elements of nature, and these elements hold together for a time to serve spirit. Nature does not enjoy her own projection.[120] The river does not drink water. The fruit tree does not eat fruit. All natural projections exist for spirit to dwell in nature. Nature acts and spirit enjoys.

Krishna states; "Actions in all cases are performed by nature, not spirit. Spirit is only the enlightener, the seer. The attributes of nature are acting with the qualities of nature, and so I am not the doer. I am only the seer."[121] The seer is our real and abiding self. Just as the sunlight causes the lotus to blossom, the light of the soul makes a body active. When the sun

---

[118] *Katha Upanishad* II.2.11.
[119] See *Tattva Samāsa* 17.
[120] Traditionally nature is designated as feminine and spirit as masculine.
[121] *Bhagavad Gītā* III.27&28.

sets, the lotus closes; when the soul departs from the body, the elements disperse. Our real self is the enlightener and observer of the instruments of action.

~~~

II-22

krtārtham prati nastam apyanastam tad anya-sādhāranatvāt
Even though the purpose of the seen is finished for the emancipated one, it does not end because the seen is universal for all others.

The purpose of the seen is to provide experience and emancipation. If truth exists, it is knowable. The movement of nature into modifications allows us to experience all truth. The faculties of intellect, ego, mind and senses are both the means of gaining knowledge through experience, and for realizing the inner truth of the seer as distinct from the seen. The *Sāmkhya Kārikā* highlights the power of the intellect for experience and enjoyment, and for discerning the subtle difference between the seer and the seen.[122]

Understanding how an all-pervasive soul manifests within the medium of *chitta* is called realization. Accepting our individual existence as one with this all-pervasive soul is emancipation. With knowledge, we shift our identification from the seen to the unbounded seer. This accomplishes the purpose of nature.

When our identification with the modifications of nature ends, we clearly discriminate between nature and spirit. Our wrong identification with nature ceases, but nature does not cease to exist. We become established in the seer and observe the movement of nature with detachment. Our identification and awareness shift from the instruments and objects of nature to the seer. All that can be seen continues to exist, but the seer is no longer defined by it.

We no longer need to associate with this or that. We shift from feeling separate and needy to knowing lasting happiness and peace. As Krishna states: "For one who is established, satisfied, and contented within the self there is nothing left to do."[123] The instruments of nature are available for the seer to use, but the attachment is severed. In this state, the intellect still discriminates, the ego still performs, the mind still collects information,

---

[122] *Sāmkhya Kārikā* XXXVII.
[123] *Bhagavad Gītā* III.17.

and the physical body still houses the subtle body. All the tools of nature keep working.

Krishna states: "Whoever is detached from this world and is attached with me, works for me and is my real devotee."[124] Even though the instruments have served their function for the one emancipated, they remain in existence for the benefit of others that are in the process of gaining knowledge.

~~~

II-23
sva-svāmi-śaktyoh svarūpopalabdhī-hetuh sanyogah
The coming together of the seer and seen (*sanyoga*) is for the realization of their true qualities and distinct powers.

The purpose of *sanyoga*, the joining together of the seer and the seen, is to realize the distinct aspects of each. Sāmkhya teaches that there are two primary qualities—principal existence and union—of any form. Principal existence means that everything in existence has two eternal, principal causes: nature and spirit. *Sanyoga* is the co-existing of these two eternal causes.

Krishna states: "Any being that is born, moving or unmoving, arises from the union of the field (nature) and the knower of the field (spirit)."[125] Nature alone cannot project, and spirit alone cannot manifest. Spirit is the inspiration for the projection of energy. When nature is enlivened by spirit, then this universe appears. These two powers are indicated as *sva*, the seen, and *svāmi*, the seer. In *sanyoga*, these two powers join to present their own form (*svarūpa*). When the two combine, the form of each distinct power can be understood.

Space is filled with electricity. Electricity is a limitless all-pervasive power, but electricity requires a medium to show its power. When electricity appears in a light bulb, it gives light. Without the bulb, we cannot see this form of light. In the same way, all-pervasive consciousness manifests through the medium of *chitta* to reveal its illumination. Our *chitta* is the projection of unmanifest energy which adopts the brilliance of consciousness: intelligence, existence, and bliss.

Above manifestation, nature and spirit are one. When they express at any level, they appear in two forms. The interplay of nature and spirit is

---

[124] *Bhagavad Gītā* XI.55.
[125] *Bhagavad Gītā* XIII.26.

explained in the story of Radha and Krishna. To understand the teaching, some new terms must be explained. *Radha* means form and it is another word for nature. Spirit is *krishna*, the attractive power. The attractive power, *krishna*, causes nature, *radha,* to accumulate into form. Attraction is countered by entropy, the repulsive power of nature, which causes things to dissipate. Attraction and repulsion create movement, and the world is always moving due to these forces.

This movement is described as dancing. In this mystical teaching, Krishna is playing the flute while Radha dances. Krishna is in the center of all movement; all around him, Radha is dancing. Nature dances in the light of spirit. Universes are coming and going always in the dance of this eternal, divine play. The dance of nature with the inspiration of spirit has always been described in mystical ways. Nature is the world of all names and forms, and spirit is the illuminating power. We are an inseparable manifestation of the divine display.

~~~

II-24
tasya hetur avidyā
The reason for that (*sanyoga*) is ignorance.

Patañjali initiated his discussion on the cause of suffering by focusing on the identification of the seer with the seen. He then described the distinct qualities of the seer and the seen. He further explained the purpose of *sanyoga* as a co-existence that reveals the qualities of these two distinct powers. Now in this *sutra*, Patañjali re-emphasizes that it is only wrong understanding that is the cause of the cognitive blending of these two powers.

The root cause of suffering is ignorance or wrong knowledge, *avidyā*. In our ignorance, we become identified with the body, the senses, the mind, ego and intellect. All are projections of nature and are changeable. When our real self becomes identified with these levels of nature, we suffer. Identification is valuing something outside the self as a quality of the self. We are seeking oneness with the self, but this can only occur when two things having the same qualities merge together. When rainwater falls into the ocean they become one and the rain cannot be separated out. If you put oil into water they can be separated because they have different qualities.

We cannot be truly united with nature. Spirit and nature have totally different qualities. They cannot be made one, but exist together. We cannot be united with nature, but we identify with nature. This identification, acceptance of nature as self, makes us feel limited, because we accept the limiting distinctions of nature. This sense of limitation due to wrong knowledge causes our suffering.

When we accept our self as allied with "this and that," then our individual soul becomes mixed with the properties of objects. This creates bondage. With correct knowledge based on direct experience we can realize our real self. With pure wisdom we can realize our individual soul, *jivatman*, is only the presence of *atman* in the medium of *chitta*. They are one, having the same qualities of existence, intelligence, and bliss.

Avidya is assigning the qualities of nature to the self. When the impressions in the intellect are accepted as the self and these properties define our existence, our ignorance takes the form of egoism. When we realize the seer and the seen are two separate powers, we experience emancipation. Ignorance of this truth causes our suffering. In order to be free, we must think carefully, seek truth, and realize it for ourselves.

~~~

II-25
tad-abhāvāt sanyogābhāvo hānam tad-drśeh kaivalyam
With the disappearance of ignorance comes the disappearance of identification. That cessation is the end of suffering and the liberation of the seer.

Krishna states: "Let the dissolution of union with pain be known as yoga."[126] *Viyoga* is the separation of that which has been united.[127] When the seer is identified with nature, we believe existence is dependent upon the modifications of nature. We believe, "this is my body, that is my job, those are my relatives, and these are my belongings." All of these beliefs held in the intellect define our existence.

There are two words that suggest union, but have very different meanings: *yoga* and *sanyoga*. In *sanyoga*, two different powers with separate qualities are blended together and they can be separated. In *yoga*, there is no togetherness; there is only oneness. Like water into water, the

---

[126] *Bhagavad Gītā* VI.23.
[127] *Tattva Samāsa* 16.

individual soul is soul, individual existence is existence, and individual consciousness is consciousness. This is *yoga*. The two are already one.

The material world cannot become attached to us; we are the ones who invest it with meaning. Our houses are never attached to us, but we are emotionally attached to our houses. If a random building burns down, the event has little meaning to us. If our own home burns, it is devastating. Thousands of people are born whom we do not celebrate; thousands die for whom we shed no tears. Our emotions are calm and our minds are steady when we have no attachment, but when we are attached, we are bound to a constant, tumultuous experience of agitation and suffering.

When we identify with external objects and experiences, we bring the properties of that relationship into our intellect. First, these properties appear as waves of thought and images called mind. Secondly, our egoistic self reacts to the stimuli by accepting or rejecting the thoughts and images based on the values and beliefs we hold. This disturbs the ability of the intellect to discriminate properly. When we relate our individual soul with these modifications, we blend the seer with the instrument of seeing.

Viyoga, separation, is the end of *sanyoga*. *Sanyoga* is the temporary union of the seer with the seen. *Viyoga* is the dissolution of this temporary union, which leads to *yoga*, the union of oneness. Yoga is about empowerment and responsibility. We have all been given the instruments necessary to gain experience and enjoy the unity of a personal and immanent experience with the source of life. The intellect is the most powerful instrument we have and it is our responsibility to use it well.

~~~

II-26
viveka-khyātir aviplavā hānopāyah
Pure, doubtless discriminative knowledge is the way to end suffering.

Hānopāyah indicates there is a method to end our suffering. This method involves *aviplavā viveka-khyātih*, the light of steady knowledge. Discriminative knowledge, *viveka*, is the clear distinction between the seer and the instrument of seeing. The values and beliefs we hold in the intellect either bind us or free us. Only by personal effort can we change how we view the world around us and how we define our self. We must implement the teachings we gain to develop keen discrimination. No other person can do this for us.

Krishna explains, "To them, who are ever steadfast in practice, I give the yoga of discrimination. Out of mere compassion for them, I become their *ātmabhava*, their inner sense of being, and by the brilliant lamp of knowledge, destroy the darkness born of ignorance." [128] With the illumination of the light of steady knowledge, we gain freedom from suffering.

The intrinsic properties of any natural phenomenon cannot be removed. Light and heat are properties of fire, and when fire is manifesting, light and heat are present. Light and heat cannot be removed from fire. If two unrelated elements mix together they can be separated and returned to their pure state. Water is liquid and cold. If we put water in contact with fire, then it becomes hot. Water boils because it adopts the qualities of fire. Heat is not a property of water, but fire's contact with water brings the quality of heat into water. Heat can be removed from water because it is not an intrinsic quality of water. One element can be temporarily influenced by the properties of another, but the foreign properties can be separated out.

The intellect, ego, mind, space, air, fire, water, and earth are projections of nature, each with its own properties and qualities. Intrinsic qualities cannot be removed from any one of these projections of nature. We cannot remove smell from earth, taste from water, heat from fire, movement from air, sound from space, thought from mind, individual existence from ego, or intelligence from intellect. However, if the quality of one is mixed with another, it can be removed. Wrong knowledge is an impurity and it can be removed.

Ignorance is not a natural property of either the seer or the seen. Misconception occurs when we accept the fluctuations of the *gunas* in nature as the seer. This gives rise to egoism. Egoism breeds feelings of me and mine in opposition to you and yours, creating attractions and aversions. As we become invested in egoism, we reinforce feelings of isolation and fear, and we suffer. When we feel separate from our own real properties, we are without discriminative knowledge.

In *sūtra* III-35, Patañjali teaches: "In the state of experience, as opposed to emancipation, there is no distinction between nature and the self. In truth they are absolutely unmixed." Nature and spirit can never be united in any state, but they appear to be united in manifestation. Patañjali

---

[128] *Bhagavd Gītā* X.10&11.

gives the example of a pure, clear crystal reflecting the redness of a nearby flower to illumine this principle.[129] When the red flower is removed, the pure clarity of the crystal can be known. When nature is enlivened, it appears that spirit is in nature, but spirit is never a part of the forms of nature. Spirit is eternally formless. The reflection of spirit in nature makes it seem that the two are one. Seeing these two clearly with pure, doubtless discriminative awareness brings the freedom from suffering called Yoga.

~~~

II-27
tasya saptadhā prānta-bhūmih prajñā
The wisdom of that realized *yogi*, at its final stage, is of seven kinds.

The goal of discriminative knowledge is the realization of the source of existence. With this realization, a *yogi* experiences the clarity and insight that is the foundation of freedom.

Seven Kinds of Wisdom	
What was necessary for knowing is known	Bondage and suffering can be avoided.
What was to be seen is seen	The cause of misery is ignorance and identification.
What was sought is obtained	Suffering can be annihilated by a method.
What is to be done is done	The method is employed to gain discriminative knowledge.
The intellect fulfilled its purpose	The modifications of *chitta* are stilled and free from desire.
Intellect and *chitta* observed independent of modifications	Impressions and projections are fully restrained. *Chitta* is seen producing the shadow of individuality.
Seer is separate from seen	Seer is free of the shadow of individuality. Emancipation is attained.

What was necessary for knowing is now known; what was to be seen is seen; what was sought is obtained; and what needed to be done is

---

[129] *Yoga Sūtras* I-41.

accomplished. The search for knowing, seeing, acquiring and achieving ends. These are the first four stages, necessary for reaching a desireless state where the *yogi* is freed from the effort of practice.

The fifth type of realization: the intellect has provided the means for gaining experience and emancipation, fulfilling its purpose. The intellect is clear and stable. In stability, a *yogi* becomes established within the self as *jivātman*. Consciousness is experienced as separate, distinct, and independent from the intellect, but not free from the influence of the *chitta*. This realization is the first of the final three stages of detachment from the instrument of seeing.

The *yogi* who realizes that the intellect emerges from impressions of experience stored near the *chitta* and governed by the three *gunas*, achieves the sixth kind of wisdom. Both the intellect and the *chitta* are observed as projections of nature. Individuality is seen as a shadow of the seer. Nature projects the medium and the self illumines and dwells as the observer of all of nature.

With the seventh type of wisdom, a *yogi* fully understands that the seer is separate from the seen. *Jivātman* is realized as the manifestation of *ātman* in the medium of *chitta*. It is *ātman* abiding as the seer—self-illumined, existent and independent of nature. This wisdom brings perfect detachment and emancipation. Everything appearing in the intellect is illumined by the self and is known clearly and completely, without distortion. This stable wisdom yields complete freedom and union with the source.

~~~

II-28
yogāngānusthānād aśuddhi-ksaye jñāna-dīptir āviveka-khyāteh
With the practice of eight-limbed yoga, impurities are destroyed and the illumination of the self culminates in discriminative knowledge.

Complete freedom is a lofty goal. In this *sūtra*, Patañjali introduces a comprehensive eight-limbed practice. *Ashtau* is eight, *anga* is limb, and *astānga yoga* is the eight-limbed path of Yoga. Regardless of our situation, we can begin to work with these guidelines and transform our lives.

There are two ways to live: practicing *yoga* or living in *bhoga*. Yoga is the awareness of the real self and the realization of oneness. *Bhoga* is the enjoyment of worldly pleasures, which leads to suffering.

The path of Yoga leads to ecstasy and divinity. We tread this path with careful honesty, decency, awareness, and consideration. If we are living in *bhoga*, by contrast, we are self-indulgent and always focused on our bodies and senses, unknowingly fueling insatiable desire. This is a self-destructive way to live, and the mindless pursuit of self-gratification ravages society and pollutes the planet.

Science and technology make life easier, and our material culture convinces us that we can fulfill our desires. We are carried away by our search for physical comfort and our belief that once we have what we want, we will be truly happy. But when we live this way, we are on a collision course with misery. As individuals, we escalate our demand for personal satisfaction; as a society, we generate increasingly toxic forms of pollution; and as a government, we intensify the development of horrific weapons. Our search for fulfillment through *bhoga* creates ceaseless desire, anxiety, and desperation.

Simply and directly, Yoga brings freedom from this suffering. Its practical methods are based on a rational assessment of life. Yoga is not a religion and it is not based on faith or belief. The science of Yoga deals with every part of human life: body, senses, mind, ego, and intellect. Beyond these and enlivening all is spirit or pure consciousness. Pollution accumulates in the intellect, ego, mind, senses, and body; but the spirit remains eternally pure. On the path of Yoga, we work to purify all five aspects of life, and our aim is to experience the eternal purity of spirit.

Yoga shows us the way to experience and realize truth. Pure knowledge is always present within, but it cannot be experienced without self-control. We must tame our desires, which spread like wildfire if we do not lead a disciplined life. *Astanga yoga* guides us toward the highest goal, uplifting others along the way.

~~~

II-29
yama-niyamāsana-prānāyāma-pratyāhāra-dhāranā-
dhyāna-samādhayo 'stāv angāni
Those eight limbs are *yama* (vows), *niyama* (observances), *āsana* (posture), *prānāyāma* (disciplined breathing), *pratyāhāra* (detachment of the senses from their objects), *dhārana* (one-pointed focus of the mind), *dhyāna* (maintained steady focus), and *samādhi* (absorption into the source).

Yoga

The *yamas* offer guidance for our social life and the *niyamas* guide our personal life. *Āsanas* and *prānāyāma* are practices that purify our physical systems and senses; *pratyāhāra* helps us control our emotions and desires; *dhāranā* develops concentration; *dhyāna* is steady contemplation of our I-amness and our source; *samādhi* is complete absorption into our source. All of these efforts and experiences are grounded in knowledge of the real self. As we realize truth, we remove our past impressions from the *chitta* and establish stability as we move forward. Through knowledge of the real self, we experience our oneness with all souls. This experience inspires selfless love and motivates actions that serve all humanity.

The *yamas* and *niyamas* are the foundation of the eight limbs. The *yamas* free us from the tangle of unhealthy interactions with others, and the *niyamas* reveal and remove the destructive ways we live within ourselves. Patañjali presents the *yamas* first.

~~~

II-30

ahimsā-satyāsteya-brahmacharyāparigrahā yamāh
The *yamas* are *ahimsā* (non-violence), *satya* (truth), *asteya* (non-stealing), *brahmacharya* (self-restraint), and *aparigraha* (non-accumulation).

Ahimsā, non-violence, is commonly accepted as the fundamental *yama*. In my opinion, non-violence is not the foundation of the five *yamas*, but comes with mastery of the other *yamas*. Hence, the first step to practice is the last one presented: non-accumulation. The tendency to accumulate initiates adultery, theft, lies, and violence. Non-accumulation, *aparigraha*, is an essential first step on the path of Yoga. If we are engrossed in the material world, we are determined to accumulate and enjoy. Our minds dwell on wealth, status and power, and we focus on what we can get rather than what we can contribute. Without even realizing it, we appropriate the resources and rights that are meant to be shared by all. Buddha recognized this truth and taught that possessions are the cause of all disturbances. When we indulge in accumulation, we cannot avoid causing harm.

We must apportion resources and save for the future. *Aparigraha* does not mean reserving nothing for ourselves, which would be impractical. Monks and people who have reached an exceptional stage of spiritual development may live in this way, but it makes sense for the rest of us to plan and save for the future. Non-accumulation teaches us not to hoard or

141

cling to our possessions. Practicing *aparigraha*, we work toward non-attachment. We refrain from coveting, do not use unfair or injurious means to obtain anything, and we maintain a healthy perspective on what we want and what we have.

Parigraha is selfish accumulation with disregard for others. The *Rig Veda* states that ignorant, greedy people obtain wealth in vain because their accumulation causes their death. Such people do not feed others; they eat sin and become sinners. In the *Bhagavad Gītā*, Krishna states that those who cook only for themselves eat sin.[130] *Parigraha* is using our resources for ourselves, alone, and hoarding what we do not need and cannot use.

Going against the current of accumulation in our materialistic society takes determined effort, but it is an effort worth making. The need to amass possessions leads to the pain of restlessness, insatiability, insecurity, defensiveness, faithlessness, and emptiness. When having things is the goal of our lives, we can never have enough because satisfying desire only breeds more desire. As desire fuels greed, we begin to use what we own to justify our importance, as well as any manner of bad behavior.

Materialism drives us to collect and hoard. The more we have, the more we want, which sets up an endless cycle of wanting and taking. This cycle wastes our lives, and fuels anxiety and selfishness. The more we have, the more we fear loss. Yoga philosophers teach us to step out of the cycle of greed and fear by simplifying our needs and developing an honest appraisal of the value of things. By gaining perspective on what we truly need, we can free ourselves of the trappings of materialism. We understand the difference between practical needs and insatiable desires. And we free ourselves from senseless taking, stock piling, protecting and fretting.

As we free ourselves from accumulation, the mind settles and we can begin to establish a meditation practice. Meditation requires the mind to focus inside. As a first step in this direction, the mind must be brought under control. If we are constantly anxious about protecting our possessions and dreaming of how to get more, quieting the mind feels impossible. Our practice of *aparigraha* supports our practice of meditation.

There is a Russian story about a man who asked a king to give him land. The king promised to grant him as much as he needed. To determine the size of his plot, the king instructed the man to set out at sunrise, walk

---

[130] *Bhagavad Gītā* III.13.

as far as he could by midday and return to the starting point at sunset. At sunrise the next morning, the greedy man began to run without stopping to rest, eat or drink. As the sun set, he ran even harder to return to the starting point, where he fell with exhaustion and died. He was buried on the small piece of land where he fell. After running the whole day, a small burial plot was all he needed.

Needs are limited, but greed has no limit. All around the world, we can see people with enormous wealth ignoring people who are starving. The tendency to build up our own wealth at another's expense occurs at every level of society. Even religious leaders fall prey to this hurtful behavior.

Our addiction to accumulation, *parigraha*, makes self-restraint, *brahmacharya*, impossible. Without self-restraint, we take from others in unethical ways and cannot practice non-stealing, *asteya*. We lie to manipulate others so we can get what we want. Even if we tell the truth, *satya*, to others, we lie to ourselves to justify our selfishness. All of these behaviors are destructive. When we allow ourselves to be carried away by *parigraha*, we cannot practice non-violence, *ahimsa*. *Aparigraha* is the fundamental practice that helps us live in keeping with the five *yamas*. When we practice these five observances, we can act in the world without causing harm.

~~~

II-31

ete jāti-deśa-kāla-samayānavacchinnāh sārva-bhaumā mahāvratam
The great vows are universal, irrespective of community, place, time, and circumstances.

From birth, we are dependent on our relationship with others, and throughout our lives we are interdependent beings. The *yamas* guide us to purify our interactions with others and build healthy relationships. All social ills can be traced to disregard for one or more of the *yamas*. Lies cause confusion and pain. Violence is destructive and leads to unimaginable grief. Stealing is unethical and it triggers fear, mistrust and hardship. A lack of self-restraint can take many forms, from promiscuity to adultery and addiction, tearing lives apart. And accumulation usurps the rights of others, while leading us on an endless, meaningless chase to acquire more.

The *yamas* are universal principles, and they are the foundation of a well-functioning society. In this *sūtra*, Patañjali points out that there is no excuse for failing to observe the *yamas*. Regardless of the moment, location, situation, or social group, we must practice these five guidelines. How we function in relationship with ourselves affects how we interact with others. Our practice of the *yamas* is supported by our practice of the *niyamas*, which purify the inner workings of our being. An established practice of the *yamas* and *niyamas* teaches us to live with integrity, both with others and with ourselves.

~~~

II-32
śauca-santosa-tapah-svādhyāyeśvara-pranidhānāni niyamāh
The five *niyamas* (observances) are *śauca* (purity), *santosa* (contentment), *tapah* (austerity), *svādhyāya* (scripture-based self-study), and *Īśvara pranidhānā* (surrender to *Īśvara*).

The *niyamas* are personal practices. If our internal environment is aligned with purity, contentment, austerity, self-awareness and divinity our actions in the external world are uplifting.

Śauca is sanctity and purity, within and without. Developing inner purity requires us to clear away our misconceptions and distractions. Outer purity relates to cleanliness. *Santosa* is contentment with our effort and requires perseverance. We practice *santosa* by giving our best effort and being satisfied with the results. When we work within our own capacity and are content with what we are able to do, we do not suffer from jealousy, self-pity, shame or resentment, and we establish safe boundaries, self-respect and self-awareness. *Tapah* means controlling our senses, emotions and minds. Our desires are powerful and compel our senses to pursue pleasures. We often feel we are at the mercy of our desires. Restraint helps us tame our desires and regain control of our lives.

Svādhyāya, self-study, is a powerful tool for transforming our lives. When we study these teachings and are ready to make lasting changes in our thinking and behavior, a lot of resistance arises. In this practice, we observe our reactions to change and become aware of our motives, thoughts, habits and patterns. When we feel desire, we can study ourselves and see that our craving is a function of the mind and ego. As we begin to assess our thoughts and actions, we can reflect on whether the things we typically think and do are truly serving ourselves and others. Self-study, guided by these teachings, helps us shift our identity away from these patterns, and towards the one who observes the patterns.

Self-study purifies the intellect. Distorted thinking pollutes the intellect and prevents us from experiencing a pure sense of self. Pollution is related with the intellect, not the seer. The seer and real self are eternally pure. When our intellect is pure, we become aware of the presence of an observer, a seer. Seeking the pure self and its connection with the source is *Iśvara praṇidhāna*. When we have stilled the modifications of the *chitta* our knowledge of truth is clear. Otherwise, egoism and our feelings of separation is the source of our misery. These *niyamas* lead us toward integrity and illuminated, discriminative knowledge. Through ethical living and refined understanding, we find and accept the seer as our real self. This is a state of expansive peace and happiness.

~~~

II-33
vitarka-bādhane pratipaksa-bhāvanam
In the practice of *yamas* and *niyamas*, when disturbed by improper thoughts, one should ponder the opposite.

Practice of the *yamas* and *niyamas* helps us become aware of the temptations and situations that drag us off the path of Yoga. When we have degrading thoughts or catch ourselves being seduced by destructive behavior, we recognize we are being lured off the path and we make a fierce effort to head back in the right direction. Without this effort, progress is impossible. We must interrupt our misguided thoughts and our harmful actions and consider the results of what we are thinking and doing. We contemplate whether we want to chase misery and run from lasting peace and happiness, or whether we are committed to choosing the opposite.

For example, if we are coveting someone else's rights or possessions, we contemplate where these thoughts will take us. We can ask ourselves, "Even if I am able to take what I want in this situation, how will my accumulation help me? Will my experience of temporary satiation bring me closer to real happiness? Does lying, cheating or stealing help me experience oneness?" By contemplating where our thoughts and actions lead, we can purify our thinking and refine our behavior. In every facet of our lives, we should examine our orientation and determine the way to stay on the path and reach our goal.

~~~

II-34
vitarkā hinsādayah krta-kāritānumoditā lobha-krodha-moha-pūrvakā mrdu-madhyādhimātrā duhkājnānānanta-phalā iti pratipaksa-bhāvanam

Actions arising out of perverse thoughts, such as violence, whether they are performed by one's self, are done for one's self by others, or are sanctioned by one's self, but done by others; these may be motivated by greed, anger, or delusion; they may be present in mild, medium or intense degree; and they are the cause of unending misery and ignorance. In this way we should ponder the opposites.

Our actions are triggered by our thoughts. How we think generates our own behavior, causes others to do things for us, and leads others to do things because of our line of thinking. When our thoughts are corrupt to any degree, our thinking causes destructive behavior; but when we purify our thoughts, our thinking inspires upliftment. Thoughts lead to actions that either help or hinder our development. Krishna states, "One should raise the self by the intellect. For the mind is either a friend or an enemy. One should not degrade oneself."[131] When we catch ourselves thinking perverse thoughts, we should make an effort to uplift our thinking.

How is it that we are endowed with such rich and varied potential, but we are stuck in suffering? We suffer simply because we are addicted to temporal pleasures. Our attachment with the material world, the body and the senses, consumes our awareness. When our desires are thwarted, we are angry. When they are satisfied, our greed and temptation increase. We use our body, senses and mind to fulfill the mind's cravings. The cycle of craving and satiation, craving and frustration, brings moments of enjoyment and ongoing suffering. When greed, ignorance, and passion fuel our thoughts and drive our actions, we bring misery into our lives. We can interrupt the cycle of suffering, and progress on the path toward eternal peace and happiness, by becoming fully aware of our unchanging source.

We cannot transform our lives without recognizing the power of our thoughts and emotions over our actions. To offer uplifting action in the world, we must channel our love toward devotion and refine our knowledge with truth. We can have knowledge that is simply information, we can feel love that is actually just passion or lust, and we can perform countless actions that serve no purpose.

---

[131] *Bhagavad Gītā* VI.5.

Transforming our thoughts, emotions and actions is a process of cultivation. We weed out anything that is undesirable from our lives, and we plant and nourish the seeds of knowledge and devotion. Our intellects collect many impressions over time. We carry numerous degrading impressions that are expressed as perverse thoughts. These undesirable thoughts lead to destructive actions. Some of our impressions are latent, and we do not become aware of them until we begin to calm the mind. This should not discourage us. Our awareness helps us along the way, even when we are disturbed by what awareness reveals. Regardless of what arises, we can continue to practice and work to remove undesirable tendencies. With steady practice and effort, we gradually realize ultimate truth and are freed from misery.

~~~

II-35
ahimsā-pratisthāyām tat-sannidhau vaira-tyāgah
In the presence of one who is established in non-violence, there is the ending of enmity.

Non-violence is not the means to an end, but the end itself. Our observation of the other four *yamas* yields *ahimsā*. When we realize the same self resides in all beings, non-violence comes naturally. With this awareness, we see that there is no difference between hurting others and hurting ourselves. Our love for all beings leads us to respect the wellbeing of others and avoid doing any harm.

Violence sprouts when we identify the self with the material world. If we are seeking selfish pleasures and dwelling on ways to increase our wealth and power, we cannot help but infringe on other people's rights and resources. Our selfish thoughts generate corrupt actions that devastate others. In this way, we tear ourselves away from happiness and peace. To banish violence from sprouting in our lives, we practice truthfulness, non-stealing, self-restraint, and non-accumulation. Our efforts foster non-violence.

In India, various sects center their teachings on non-violence. Historically, this emphasis disempowered the people and government of India, which led to occupation by outside powers for eleven hundred years. The Vedas do not teach victimization. They favor realism over idealism, and define violence as behavior motivated by greed, hatred, arrogance and

147

dishonesty. The judicious use of force to oppose malicious violence and corruption is needed.

Patañjali teaches that we should remain neutral around corrupt people and avoid them if possible. They do not warrant our empathy and they do not deserve our support. But when vicious people are abusing others, they must be stopped. By stopping violence, we serve those who have been abused and we save the offenders from themselves. Immoral domination creates strong impressions in the perpetrator, and these impressions lead to suffering. Ending and preventing violence safeguards society and protects violent people from their own destruction.

According to the *Dharmasāstra*,[132] a king becomes responsible for the sins of sinners if they are not properly punished. Aligned with this principle, Krishna directs Arjuna to fight his evil adversaries, because it is his duty to society. "Take happiness and loss, victory and defeat as alike. Join the battle; in this way you will not incur sin."[133] If we engage in fighting to protect ourselves and others from corruption and cruelty, we are honoring the practice of non-violence.

Ahimsa is a fundamental tenet of Yoga. The practice of non-violence reaches fruition when we are established in the real self. In this state, our actions are inspired by joy, generosity and devotional love. Patañjali indicates that when we achieve this level of *ahimsa*, our peaceful presence disarms everyone around us.

~~~

II-36
satya-pratisthāyām kriyā-phalāśrayatvam
Established in truthfulness, the words of a *yogi* come to fruition.

According to Yoga philosophy, the eternal is truth and is called the real, *sat*, while everything that changes is untruth, and is called unreal, *asat*. Therefore, manifest nature is untruth. It is not eternal and cannot provide stable inner peace and happiness. This does not suggest that the material world is an illusion; it exists. But philosophically, eternal knowledge and bliss are real because they are abiding truth.

---

[132] *Dharmasāstra* is a summary of religious, ethical and legal principles. The *Dharmasāstra* derives its authority from the Vedas, though few, if any, of the contents can be directly linked with Vedic texts.
[133] *Bhagavad Gītā* II.38.

Our lives consist of both the changeable and the non-changeable. The gross, subtle and causal bodies are temporal. The physical body, senses and mind comprise the gross body. The ego and the *tanmatras* form the subtle body, and the *chitta* is the causal body.[134] All three bodies are subject to change because they are projections of nature. The eternal aspect of human life is the seer, the real truth of our lives. We can experience, realize, and know the seer, which appears as our existence and awareness. The seer remains unchanging throughout our lives.

Truth is more than honesty. In Yoga, truth is unchanging oneness. When we are not living aligned with truth, we are identified with nature and suffer through incessant change and the cycles of birth and death. In our misidentification, we tumble through countless fluctuations; we become weak, confused, corrupt and unstable. We find our footing when we lift our minds toward pure consciousness and unite with the real self. As we begin to discriminate clearly, we are able to realize and know truth. Established in ultimate truth, a *yogi's* efforts bear fruit.

~~~

II-37
asteya-pratisthāyām sarva-ratnopasthānam
The establishment of non-stealing brings prosperity.

Asteya is non-stealing, which means more than not taking; it is an attitude of not desiring what belongs to others. With this in mind, accumulation is a form of stealing. Wasting resources, taking credit for another's work, and slander are also theft.

The *Bhagavad Gītā* encourages us to perform action motivated by sacrifice, without attachment to the results of our actions.[135] Non-stealing includes recognizing our reliance on others for everything, from the things we use, the food we eat, and the lessons we learn, to the opportunities and guidance we receive. If we do not appreciate our providers, caregivers, teachers, and divine inspiration, we are stealing. We steal any time we deny what rightfully belongs to others.

Truth can only be realized when we stand firmly on the foundation of non-stealing. If we are focused on accumulation and engaged in taking the rights of others, our minds are disturbed and we cannot know peace. We must realize that there is no division between our spiritual lives and our

134 See *Yoga Sūtras* II-19.
135 *Bhagavad Gītā* IV.28 through 33.

secular lives. We will never realize truth or gain stable wisdom without practicing self-control. Only when we remove our tendencies to steal in any form, do we experience contentment, pure wisdom, and peace. Our steady observation of *asteya* supports our realization of the self and our source in ultimate reality.

When we are established in non-stealing, we prosper and are freed from desiring anything that traps us in the material world. *Ahāra* is everything we receive in life, and *vihāra* is what we offer. Any time we distort *ahara* with unethical enjoyment, we disturb the *chitta* and make it impure. And any time we tell lies or act with violence, we degrade our *vihāra*, causing more pollution in the *chitta*. We clear away these impurities by observing the five interwoven vows. Our purification of the *chitta* leads to an unshakeable memory and our establishment in truth.

~~~

II-38
brahmacarya-pratisthāyām vīrya-lābhah
With establishment in *brahmacharya* (self-restraint), there is preservation of energy.

Brahmacharya is often considered celibacy or sexual restraint, but it is more than the moderation of sexual behavior. All of the cognitive and active senses must be controlled. When we let our senses control our minds, the senses lead us to enjoy external experiences. Desire feeds on desire, and we become enslaved by our senses.

Mind is the movement of ego. When the ego moves toward an object, the mind possesses the qualities of the object in the form of waves of thought. This possessive and determinative quality is called mind. The mind's sense of entitlement and ownership grows when our thoughts are dominated by the stimulation of the senses. We cannot control the mind without controlling our senses.

Brahmacharya is often misunderstood. Mental and emotional restraint is much more powerful than physical self-control. And we cannot simply suppress our desires. The more we try to suppress a feeling, the more dangerous it grows. The more we avoid thinking about something, the more that thought takes root in our minds. *Brahmacharya* is not forced restraint of physical action, and it is not the suppression of desire. It is the process of establishing our inner connection with the seer.

Brahmacharya is often reduced to the physical restraint of the body. Throughout history, this misunderstanding has led to the subjugation of women. Women were considered a hindrance and had to be avoided by those ostensibly practicing *brahmacharya*. This is a senseless idea based on a misinterpretation. The path of Yoga is equally available to men and women. According to the Vedas, the soul is neither male nor female. A true *brahmachari* visualizes oneness in all and sees all souls as the self. *Brahmacharya* leads to oneness with the supreme, and self-control arises with freedom from the desire to possess. This restraint is to be observed by both men and women and permeates both the body and the mind.

Krishna tells us that external control of the senses while letting the mind dwell on the objects of the senses is hypocrisy.[136] We practice self-restraint by controlling the outward flow of the senses while internally devoting our passion toward the source of self. We must discriminate between the degrading results from unethical sensual experiences and the abiding joy we feel when we experience oneness with the source of life. Only this experience of oneness with our source satisfies our inner demand for happiness.

Practicing *brahmacharya*, we increase our *vīrya*: vigor, life energy, and courage. *Vīrya* does not come with control of our sexual energy alone. Control of all our organs of sense, including the mind, develops the determination, stamina and fortitude we need to progress toward *samādhi*.

~~~

II-39
aparigraha-sthairye janma-kathantā-sambodhah
After achieving stability in non-accumulation, the *yogi* becomes aware of many lives both past and future.

Attachment and accumulation go hand in hand. A firm commitment to non-accumulation releases attachment and brings the senses under control. When the senses cease their clamoring for satisfaction, the mind is free from distractions and can function with pure reason, wisdom and a realization of the source of life. This purifies the *chitta* and allows insights to come forward. At this level of purified awareness, the origins and results of our impressions from past lives may be revealed. These insights

---

[136] *Bhagavad Gītā* III.6.

offer guidance because these impressions in the *chitta* give results in future lives.

We do not have to wait for these insights to root out our impressions. Pure consciousness manifests in the medium of the individual *chitta*, which is our individual soul. Under the dark influence of ignorance, our souls become infatuated with nature and feel separate from the source of life. This identification of the seer with nature, in the form of the intellect, breeds egoism, *asmitā*. Our misidentification produces attachments, aversions, anxiety and the fear of death.

Egoism creates desires. When we satisfy our desires, we feel temporary pleasure. This momentary release fuels greater attraction, which creates the tendency to accumulate and hoard. When our desires are frustrated, we feel anger and many other forms of aversion. Our desire to hold onto everything we have creates fear, and our greatest fear is the fear of death.

To free ourselves from this tumultuous race to have and to hoard, we must control our minds and our senses, and rein in our desires. We must observe what it is we are chasing and what we are getting for our efforts. As we turn away from finite material gain and toward lasting peace and happiness, we work in our own unique way. We are the ones who have set the traps that ensnare us, and we must search out and disarm our own pitfalls.

Along the way, we can enjoy comfort, but our simple enjoyment is guided by need, not driven by desire. Our enjoyment is tempered by consideration for others, and we avoid taking pleasure at another person's expense. Our awareness that egoism triggers feelings of separation and causes our desire to accumulate guides us to practice non-accumulation as we search for the source of self. Suffering originates from our misguided sense of separation, and we invite more suffering with our desire to accumulate. Through practice of the *yamas*, we remove our habit of accumulation. We refine our efforts with a disciplined personal practice of the *niyamas*.

~~~

II-40
śaucāt svānga-jugupsā parair asansargah
With purity, there develops a disinterest for one's own organs and a disinclination for physical contact with others.

Yoga

II-41
sattva-śuddhi-saumanasyaikāgryendriya-jayātma-darśana-yogyatvāni ca

Purity leads to a clear and cheerful mind, one-pointedness, control of the senses, and the ability to realize one's own self.

The first *niyama* is *śauca*, purity. Purity applies to every aspect of our lives, from what we eat and drink to our hygiene, interactions, speech, work and behavior. A clean body, a vegetarian diet, honesty, pure thoughts, and ethical actions are all aspects of the practice of purity.

We often overvalue physical strength and energy. A healthy mind is significantly more uplifting than a healthy body. The mind can create sanctity. When we focus on developing a stable mind and seek upliftment for ourselves and others, we lose our fixation on our bodies and physical contact.

This level of mental purity is not possible without a pure diet. The mind is formed by the food we eat. As food is digested, it is processed into fluids that become the blood, flesh, fat, bone, bone marrow, reproductive cells, and finally *ojas*. According to Ayurveda, *ojas* is the result of the complete digestion of food and it is the juice of vitality in the body. When there is sufficient *ojas* in the body we have healthy immunities and when *ojas* is deficient there is weakness and fatigue. The mind reflects this state of sufficiency or deficiency.

Purity is both internal and external. Everything we do, within and without, is connected with our devotional practices and spiritual existence. The purity of *chitta* is the core of our spiritual life. A purified *chitta* is the internal sanctuary that provides peace of mind, concentration, control of the senses, and the ability to realize one's own self.

~~~

II-42
santosād anuttamah sukha-lābhah

Contentment brings incomparable happiness.

Santosa is satisfaction or contentment, but this *sūtra* does not encourage complacency or laziness. Patañjali teaches us to use our energy and abilities to uplift ourselves and serve others. He encourages us to give steadily our best effort, and then to be always content with the outcome. When we are satisfied with the results of our actions, whatever they may be, we feel no need to harm or take from others.

153

We are provided with bodies, strength and consciousness. We must use these blessings and make our contribution in the world. Practicing contentment is not resting but rather is making the best of what is offered to us by others. The Russian writer, Leo Tolstoy tells that he was once sitting on a park bench when a boy approached him.

"Please, sir, a few kopecks," the boy said, holding out his hand.

For a long time, Tolstoy just looked at the boy and said nothing. Finally, he asked, "Why are you begging?"

The boy dropped his hand. "I am poor. I have nothing. My family has trouble finding food."

Tolstoy looked at the boy's hands and said, "I can give you twenty thousand rubles for one of your hands."

The boy looked down at his two hands.

"Or I can give you the same amount for one of your eyes, or legs. You can manage with one, and you will be very rich if you sell the other."

The boy refused and walked off, but he understood the value of what Tolstoy taught him. A few years later, he returned as a rich man and found Tolstoy sitting in the same garden. Tolstoy did not recognize him. The man greeted Tolstoy and told him that he was the young beggar who had received a lesson on the value of his assets. He had put them to good use and was no longer a hungry beggar.

We have numerous assets and means provided by the divine power of nature. When we use them guided by wisdom and inspired by service, we can be content with the results of our work. We enjoy whatever we create or earn, knowing that our ultimate goal is beyond the work of our hands and the rewards of our status or wealth. Yoga philosophy describes four achievements in life: virtue, knowledge, detachment, and prosperity. We can achieve these four without great wealth or fame, but a wealthy, famous person may not have any of these achievements. Without detachment, they will never feel prosperous enough. A detached person is able to enjoy wealth and peace of mind. Detachment is a great ideal, and we can achieve it in the light of knowledge, which dawns in a virtuous life. Prosperity is the result of detachment, detachment comes from knowledge, and knowledge dawns with virtue.

~~~

II-43

kāyendriya-siddhir aśuddhi-ksayāt tapasah
Austerity diminishes impurity and brings the power of control over the body and senses.

Tapah is often thought of as tolerating difficulty on the way to fulfilling our duties. According to the Upanishads, *tapah* means considering right from wrong and continuing to do the right thing, even in the face of obstacles. Patañjali indicates that austerity develops strong faith and the ability to face difficulties. The practice of *tapah* includes fasting, physical postures, breathing practices, and other *hatha yoga* cleansing exercises to purify the body, senses, and mind. Ultimately, *tapah* involves managing our emotions.

Emotions flow like a river, and they can be channeled and put to good use. We should try to keep our emotions from flooding toward the senses and instead divert them toward the supreme cause. When we exercise this control, we become alert and powerful, conserving our energy and building up fortitude. This strength is beneficial for continuing on the path in the midst of the challenges we face in daily life. The power we generate with austerity helps us navigate our lives within our families, our jobs, and our communities; austerity helps us persevere in these roles, guided by the light of spirit.

As we regain control of our emotions, we are able to master our senses. Just as fire can be useful or dangerous, the senses are useful when they are controlled, but dangerous when used carelessly. With austerity, we skillfully manage our emotions and gain control of our senses. As masters of our emotions and senses, we establish the right conditions for purity in the mind.

~~~

II-44

svādhyāyād ista-devatā-samprayogah
Self-study guided by scriptures and *mantra* brings a vision of the chosen object of worship.

Svādhyāya is self-study or introspection. In the practice of self-study, we observe our actions and probe our motivations to determine the value of our thoughts and behaviors. As we develop awareness of the value and consequences of our actions, we begin to refine our motives and choose our actions more consciously, and our actions become more beneficial. As

155

we analyze our purposes and goals, our actions shift toward service to all. Working to purify ourselves and serve others, without desiring results from our actions, we experience contentment and choose lasting happiness over trouble and suffering.

Exploring the self with intellect and wisdom, we naturally turn inside. Introspection is a useful tool in practice and in daily life. Working with *svādhyāya,* we gain perspective and can evaluate our motives, thoughts and behaviors. When we feel greedy or manipulative, we can ask, "What am I chasing and how am I trying to get it? Am I sacrificing my integrity to get something that ultimately has no value?" This kind of assessment helps us balance and control our emotions and actions. With perspective, we relinquish accumulation and establish a much greater goal for our lives.

The teachings from scriptures and the guiding light of *mantra* are essential aspects of self-study. Scriptures offer the map for charting our path, and *mantra* creates a vibration that is the essence of our destination.

~~~

II-45
samādhi-siddhir īśvara-pranidhānāt
With surrender to *Īśvara* comes achievement of *samādhi.*

Introspection gradually lifts us into the realization of our source. Life does not cause life. Everything in existence is an effect of *Īśvara*, God. God lives within us in the form of our own self. As we seek to find the self, we are seeking this source. God is always with us. Just as an emerging ray of sun cannot exist separate from the sun, we cannot exist separate from God. We have many different names for this supreme cause, but the source of our lives is one. This one infinite cause is the source of our strength, knowledge, and power.

As spirit is pure, the real self of all beings is pure. When we realize oneness with the supreme cause, we lose our feelings of separation and limitation. Truly, none of us is finite or limited. We are all one with the supreme cause. Upon realizing this oneness, we experience a feeling of perfection and freedom. This experience removes any feelings of deficiency that burden us when we live in ignorance. Understanding that we are a projection of the supreme source helps us to achieve a stable, even state of intellect. Living with awareness of the truth of our existence, we surrender to *Īśvara*.

~~~

156

II-46
sthira-sukham āsanam
The comfortable and stable seat is *āsana.*

We need strong, supple bodies as we begin to establish a meditation practice. Sitting in quiet awareness also requires a calm nervous system, a peaceful mind and a one-pointed focus. Physical yoga practices, *asana,* and breathing practices, *prānāyāma,* help us build strong, flexible bodies, quiet our nerves, and focus our minds internally. Tulsidas stated, "Without a doubt, the body is the first and foremost means of the divine practices."[137]

Āsana brings strength, firmness, and elasticity in the body, and alleviates discomfort and disease. Even a small number of yoga poses serve to maintain supple stability in the body and mind. The three basic movements of extending, flexing and twisting the body benefit our anatomical and physiological systems. These physical practices provide a sense of wellbeing on more than just a physical level. For example, *asana* practice balances the endocrine system, which is particularly important for the mental and intellectual balance that supports meditation.

In addition to postures, *hatha yoga*[138] includes *mudras, bandhas, neti, trātaka* and other practices. *Mudras* or seals contain life energy through body and hand gestures. A common *mudra* for meditation is *dhyāna mudra,* created by resting one palm in the other with thumbs lightly touching. The three *bandhas* are internal root, abdomen and chin holds that assist the vital flow and containment of *prāna,*[139] the five types of life energy. *Hatha yoga* is sometimes taught with a sequence of cleansing practices, *neti,* and concentration techniques, *trātaka.* The complete range of *hatha* practices is extensive, but we can receive tremendous benefits without practicing every method. By establishing a regular and evolving practice, we align our lives with flourishing physical health and mental wellbeing, while strengthening our conscious connection with the source of life.

Practicing *asana* is like taming a lion. A lion is not tamed in one day. This work is done slowly, gently, intelligently and lovingly. As with lion taming, if we use harsh tactics we put ourselves in danger. When we keep our *hatha yoga* practice appropriate and safe, it is powerfully beneficial.

---

[137] *Rāmāyana* VI-96.
[138] See II-48 for description of *hatha yoga.*
[139] See *Yoga Sūtras* II-49.

Patañjali suggests simplicity and encourages us to work with *āsana* to support a comfortable, stable practice of meditation.

~~~

II-47
prayatna-śaithilyānanta-samāpattibhyām
With relaxation of effort and meditation on the infinite, the postures are perfected.

Prayatna-śithilya is releasing the natural tendency toward intensity in action and movement; and *ananta-samāpatti* is absorption into the infinite. Yoga postures should be explored with quiet attention, rather than force or impatience. Meditation on the infinite further stills the body and calms the mind. This quiet state of the gross and subtle bodies makes the posture firm, comfortable, and stable. When physical distractions are quieted, we are able to maintain a stable seat with a steady internal focus.

Yoga āsanas are both physical and mental practices. As we move the body, every movement should be linked with thought and breath. Two kinds of movement are initiated when the *chitta* is enlightened by pure consciousness: breath and thought. Breath and thought are twins. The principles of *hatha yoga* teach that if we control our breath, we can control our thoughts. *Raja yoga* emphasizes the thought process, reasoning that if we control our thoughts, we automatically control our breath. The former method aims to control the breath to settle the mind, while the latter aims to control the mind to settle the breath.

Dominion over thought and breath frees us from desire. Desire is stimulated by signals from the cognitive senses. The senses are called *buddhi indriya*, meaning they provide information that is relayed to the intellect. The cognitive senses are related with thought and the desires of the mind. The active senses are related with action and the movement of breath.[140] Uncontrolled, our thought and breath are engaged with satisfying desire. When we desire something, our thoughts of craving inspire our active senses to obtain the object of desire, and our breath makes our actions possible. All activities are related with thought and breath.

In *āsana* practice, movement should be explored with and guided by thought and breath. Two systems in the body correspond with thought and breath. The nervous system is related with thought, and the circulatory

---

[140] The cognitive senses are smell, taste, form, touch, and hearing. The active senses are walking, grasping, swallowing/talking, procreating, and eliminating.

system is related with breath. As we focus the mind on movement and fuel movement with breath, we soothe our nerves and support healthy circulation, bringing peaceful awareness and vitality into every level of our being. *Asana* practice is a powerful method for releasing blocked energy and relieving stiffness in the body, as well as sparking awareness and attention in the mind. The awareness that we develop in *asana* practice, as we attend to the body, breath and mind, serves us in every facet of life.

As we move the body through *asanas*, we develop an appreciation for thought and breath as manifestations of the source of life. In this way, we work with the body and we reach into infinity. If we let our minds wander as we explore a posture, we are wasting an opportunity to experience consciousness. It is easy to move in a habitual way when practicing *asana*, or to compare ourselves with others when we are in a class setting. Again and again, we must return to an internal focus, and attend to the value of the pose. As we engage with intentional movement, an awakened mind and nourishing breath, we reach toward our source with ease.

~~~

II-48
tato dvandvānabhighātah
With the perfection of *āsana*, the *yogi* is not afflicted by the dualities.

Hatha comes from the root terms, *ha*, sun, and *tha*, moon. *Hatha Yoga* practice balances the body between heating and cooling, bringing the opposing elements of fire and water into equilibrium.

If *rajoguna* and *tamoguna* work in the light of *sattoguna*, then we experience wellbeing. When *rajoguna* dominates, we experience agitation and anxiety. When *tamoguna* becomes more powerful, we feel sluggish, lazy and depressed. When we balance the opposing forces in the body, we develop an awareness of harmony that serves us in the larger world. Balance of our inner environment leads to acceptance of the outer environment. When we establish steady, quiet, attentive action in *asana*, we become less reactive and maintain equanimity as nature changes.

~~~

159

II-49
tasmin sati īvāsa-prasvāsayor gati-vicchedah prānāyāmah
**After stability in the postures, control of inhalation and
exhalation is *prānāyāma*.**

Patañjali indicates that breathing practices, *prānāyāma*, are to be
performed only after the postures have established stability. *Asana* practice
calms the nervous system, brings vitality to the circulatory system,
strengthens and stretches the tissues, improves digestion, and balances the
endocrine system, thus preparing the body for breathing practices.

In *prānāyāma*, *ha* refers to the heating quality of the inhalation, and *tha*
refers to the cooling quality of the exhalation. *Ha*, the in-breath draws
oxygen into the body. *Tha*, the out-breath discharges carbon dioxide and
toxins. There are many variations of *prānāyāma*. For example, *bhastrikā*,
forceful belly breathing, helps awaken the life energy that lies dormant in
the lowest *chakra* of the body. With *sūrya bhedana* and *chandra bhedana*, we
increase or decrease the heat in the body. In *nādī śodhāna*, we balance the
two sides of the body by breathing through alternate nostrils. Breathing
practices deepen the effects of *āsana*, and quiet the nervous system,
preparing us for the inward focus of meditation.

Prāna is the vital force of life energy in the body. There are five types
of *prāna* circulation.[141] The first, also called *prāna*, is inhalation, which
stimulates an ascending energy. *Apāna* is exhalation, which stimulates a
descending energy. *Samāna* is the heat of digestion. *Vyāna* pervades the
whole body and supports blood circulation. And *udāna* moves between the
throat and the head, nourishing the glands and the brain.

In the Vedas we read that there are seven sentinels who protect the
city of the body. These seven guards include the five cognitive senses and
prāna and *apāna*, which are the essential ascending and descending breaths.
Among these seven, *prāna* and *apāna* never sleep. In deep sleep, we are
unconscious and the five senses do not function. But *prāna* and *apāna* are
always awake, protecting and watching over us. We are unconscious in
deep sleep, but we remain alive because of the movement of *prāna* and
apāna. When breathing ceases, our life force has left the body.

Prānāyāma practices establish evenness of inhalation and exhalation.
Control and balance of our life energy is *hatha yoga*.

~~~

---

[141] See also *Tattva Samāsa* 10.

II-50
bāhyābhyantara-stambha-vrttir deśa-kāla-sankhyābhih-paridrsto dīrgha-sūksmah
The depth and subtlety of *prānāyāma* depends on the placement, length of time, and number of the exhalation, inhalation and retention inside.

Breathing has three phases. *Rechaka* is exhalation, *pūraka* is inhalation, and *kumbhaka* is breath retention. Retention is of two kinds, external and internal. In external *kumbhaka*, the breath is held out, and in internal *kumbhaka*, it is held in, both with *bandhas*. A *hatha yogi* is a master of *prānāyāma* and controls the mind through controlled breathing. A *raj yogi* controls breathing through a disciplined mind. For many of us, it is easier to work with the breath than with the mind. Focusing our full attention on the breath slowly leads us to the real self in the *brahma chakra*.

Many of us are familiar with the eight *chakras* in the body: five along the spine, one in the palate, one between the eyes, and one at the top of the head. The eighth *chakra* is the *brahma chakra*. Less commonly known is the ninth *chakra*, *vyomachakra*. This ninth *chakra* is beyond the body, and it holds the body in place like a root. In the *Bhagavad Gītā*, the body is likened to an upside-down tree with its roots above the head in space.[142] The body is rooted in the *vyomachakra*, the ninth *chakra*. This is the point where energy and spirit come to work together. There we find the source of thought and breath.

Breath control requires knowledge of the *bandhas*. In the practice of *uddīyāna bandha*, the abdominal hold, air is completely exhaled from the lungs. As the air is forced out, the abdomen draws in toward the spine and up under the ribs. The pelvic floor is lifted in *mūla bandha*, the root hold. The head bends forward and the chin tucks over the thyroid to create *jālandhara bandha*, the chin hold. The three *bandhas* can be used together to retain the air out. When they are released, air rushes in, filling the body with oxygen. This practice amplifies life energy and elevates *prāna* for meditation. Retention of the out-breath cleanses the body and soothes the mind. Retention of the in-breath strengthens *udāna prāna* and supports awareness in meditation, and it is held without *uddīyāna bandha*.

Breathing practices differ because of the emphasis of placement in the body, the length of breaths, the holds, and the numbers of cycles.

---

142 *Bhagavad Gītā* XV.1-3.

Powerful changes occur when the *bandhas* are practiced between rounds of deep breathing, in conjunction with *mantra* and a careful diet. The increased sensitivity that comes with these practices has led many *yogis* to prefer solitude, but a powerful practice can be carefully moderated to support daily life.

~~~

II-51

bāhyābhyantara-visayāksepī caturthah
The elevation of *prāna* that transcends the mental association with inhalation and exhalation is the fourth.

In normal waking activity, our awareness and *prāna* are active with our physical body and senses. The outward flow of *prāna* enlivens our senses, enabling them to collect information from everything around us. We see, hear, smell, taste, touch, grasp and hold objects, speak, talk and walk. When we make contact with something we desire, we enjoy ourselves and *prāna* is enlivened. All of these activities expend our life energy as they stimulate the inhalation and exhalation of our breath. Throughout regular life, breathing, which supports all of our actions, is activated, quickened and shortened. Our breathing is constantly fluctuating, but we are mostly unaware of this and we do not realize how it affects our level of energy and our ability to function.

Prānāyāma practice helps us to reclaim conscious control over our breathing, which benefits every level of our existence. As we become proficient in *prānāyāma*, our inhalations and exhalations become long and subtle. As we establish mastery over our breathing process, we suspend the outward flow of *prāna* escaping through our actions and our senses. *Udana prāna* contains and elevates our breathing within the intellect, ego and mind. The containment of breath in ascension gradually leads to a suspension of breath. This fourth experience of *prāna* is an illuminating state of elevation.

We cannot practice this state, as it is an experience of grace, but we can practice *prānāyāma* to prepare ourselves for this experience. We actively and consciously practice the extension and suspension of breath. Gradually, our awareness shifts away from the external world and our *prāna* is less agitated. In time, *prāna* returns to an internal state of resting with the seer. In this process, *rajoguna* and *tamoguna* cede their tendencies and *sattoguna* has dominion.

162

~~~

II-52
tatah ksīyate prakāśāvaranam
Then the veil covering the supreme light is dispersed.

With the practices of *pranāyāma*, inertia and restlessness are removed from the mind. The *tamasic* coverings of dullness, doubt, indolence, and laziness, and the *rajasic* exertions of pride, desire, anger, passion, lust, and greed, which had been shrouding illumination, are diminished and temporarily dissipate.

When our *prāna* returns to the epicenter of the *chitta*, the modifications of intellect, ego, and mind quiet. These modifications have obstructed our awareness and veiled our experience, of the seer. When our thoughts and breath quiet, the supreme light of the seer is able to witness the instrument of seeing, the intellect. In this state, we have an experience that is separate from our identity with the objects of the senses.

~~~

II-53
dhāranāsu ca yogyatā manasah
There is the complete ability to focus the mind.

Pranāyāma practices elevate our vital life energy away from the objects of the senses. When the mind disengages from focusing on external objects and the memories of sense experiences subside, distracting thoughts and images diminish. When agitating thoughts subside, the presence of the seer, free from these limitations, fills the mind with an awareness of existence separate from a limited identity. When we are aware that we have shifted to the observer, the mind can be guided by the intellect and we gain the ability to focus on one point.

When we develop the ability to concentrate the mind internally with a one-pointed focus, the mind withdraws its external activity. Gradually, the veil covering the seer is lifted.

~~~

II-54
sva-visayāsamprayoge cittasya svarūpānukāra ivendriyānām pratyāhārah
Ceasing contact of the *chitta* and the senses with their objects, and establishing identification with the source is *pratyāhāra.*

Ahāra refers to everything we receive through the senses. We can think of *ahāra* as the food for the senses, everything that we take in through the senses. *Pratyāhara* is withdrawing the senses from the objects of the senses. To practice *pratyāhara*, we must control our emotions and desires. Desire for stimulation naturally draws our attention outward. Our eyes, ears, tongue, nose, and skin search out and collect information from the things they can see, hear, taste, smell and touch. Unchecked, desire always intensifies and drives the senses to seek stimulation. *Pratyāhara* is reining in the senses and turning them away from the things that feed them.

Krishna states that if the mind follows the wandering senses, then a person's wisdom will be carried away as a turbulent wind carries away a boat on the water.[143] A single sense, when lured by its object, diverts our attention; every experience is compounded because it involves many senses. As a cool breeze touches the skin, it also rustles leaves, carries a scent and creates visible movement. Sensual experience may trigger fond or fearful memories that preoccupy us.

Attachment to the senses breeds the fluctuations of joy and aversion, with favorable and unfavorable experiences.[144] When we have a pleasing experience, we seek it again and again, and suffer when we are without it. When we have a negative experience, we avoid it, but live in fear of it even when it is not with us. When we turn our senses from their objects and control our mind's movement, we bring the mind under the direction of the intellect. This is *pratyāhara*.

The *Katha Upanishad* teaches that the individual soul is like a rider in a chariot. "Know the individual soul as the rider of the chariot of the body, the intellect as the charioteer, and the mind as the reins.[145] The senses are like horses and the objects are the paths on which they tread."[146] The horses pull the chariot, but the charioteer directs the horses with the reins.

---

[143] *Bhagavad Gītā* II.67.

[144] *Bhagavad Gītā* V.22.

[145] When chariots were used, a driver, or charioteer, held the reins, while the owner rode as a passenger.

[146] *Katha Upanishad* I.3.3 and 4.

164

If the charioteer is a poor driver or is ignorant of the destination, the horses are uncontrolled and make no progress toward a specific place. The unrestrained horses will run to eat the green grass off the path, and the owner and charioteer will be dislodged from the chariot. When the senses and the mind are controlled by the intellect, the mind steadily reins in the senses. In the *Bhagavad Gītā*, Krishna gives the image of a tortoise. As a tortoise withdraws his limbs, we can withdraw our senses from the objects of the senses, and develop stable wisdom.[147]

Breathing exercises prepare us for *pratyāhāra*. Through *prāṇāyāma*, we lift our *prāṇa* away from enlivening the senses and experience a more expansive sense of self. Divinity is within us, next to our intellect. When we withdraw the senses in *pratyāhāra*, we begin our search for the seer.[148]

~~~

II-55
tatah paramā vaśyatendriyānām
Then there is the complete control of the senses.

Pratyāhāra is the transitional phase from the practices that involve external effort to the practices that are deeply internal. The first five limbs of *aṣṭāṅga yoga*: *yama*, *niyama*, *āsana*, *prāṇāyāma*, and *pratyāhāra*, prepare us for the last three limbs of *dhāraṇā*, *dhyāna*, and *samādhi*. *Pratyāhāra* is a prerequisite for concentration. When our minds become one-pointed, we are in a state of *dhāraṇā*, concentration. With concentration, we can move into *dhyāna*, meditation.

With control of the senses, we engage the senses in doing what needs to be done, rather than for self-indulgence. Turning inside does not mean that we leave society. We are social beings and we live within families and communities. Life with others is made up of give and take; time for dedicated practice and time with others. In leading a divine life, we live peacefully within ourselves and with each other, and every aspect of life is a form of devotion.

Our interest in living peacefully develops gradually. As we grow disillusioned with accumulation, we become curious about the meaning and source of our life, and we begin a deeper, more internal search. We turn away from sensual contentment and achievements; our identity shifts from the body and its surroundings toward the seer. We begin to see that

---

147 *Bhagavad Gītā* II.57&58.
148 *Katha Upanishad* II.1.1.

our habits and dispositions that were produced by our ignorance have led us into unhealthy attachments and destructive behaviors, and have wasted our abilities and strength. As we develop healthier behaviors and loosen the grip of our attachments, our capacity and power increase. Knowledge, virtue, detachment and determination help us move forward.

With the effort of concentration and the practice and experience of meditation, we attain complete control of the senses, and we move toward oneness with spirit. Established in pure knowledge and bliss, we eventually reach *samadhi*.

~~~

Section III—*Vibhūti Pada*
Accomplishments

The final three limbs of *astānga yoga* are presented in the beginning of section III, *Vibhūti Pada*. *Vibhūti* means accomplishment, including supernormal powers. Patañjali provides a warning in III-37 explaining that, "These powers are obstacles in the way of *samādhi*, but are powers in an outwardly focused mind." Some powers may appear naturally with the deeper practices, but they often distract practitioners from the attainment of the highest goal. Since this text focuses on the philosophy and methods of Yoga as the means for attaining liberation and removing suffering, only *dhāranā*, *dhyāna*, and *samādhi* are emphasized as they are part of the eight-limbed path. In the closing of *Vibhūti Pada*,[149] Patañjali will describe *kaivalya*, liberation, as the equal purity of *sattva* and *purusha*. Here, *sattva* indicates a quiet medium in which the seer resides in its own purity. Every one of us has the means to experience this state of unity with the source of life.

Yoga Sūtras II-10 & 11 advises us to end the subtle root cause of pain with the practice of inverse propagation. This is accomplished through meditation. Meditation includes three phases. First is the development of mental concentration on a specific point called *dhāranā*. The second phase is the uninterrupted continuity of contemplative thought called *dhyāna*. The third stage, where the *chitta* reflects the object alone as if devoid of its own identity, is called *samādhi* or absorption.

We form latent impressions by collecting experiences through the organs of the senses and perception, and we create a self-identity based on these experiences. Inverse propagation is the process of working backwards through these layers of impressions and attachments. By virtue of carefully addressing our attachments at each stage, we understand the workings of *prakriti* and come to realize the seer as distinct from this activity

Here at the beginning of the third *pada*, *dhāranā*, *dhyāna*, and *samādhi* are considered three parts of *samyama*,[150] the ability to hold or restrain one's

---

[149] *Yoga Sūtras* III-55.
[150] *Yoga Sūtras* III-4.

impulses from moving away from the observed or known object. Mastering this process brings lucidity of consciousness—the light of knowledge, pure discrimination.[151] *Samyama* is to be practiced in stages to unwind deeper and deeper layers of misidentification.[152]

To be established in Yoga, we must quiet the modifications of *chitta*. The seer is self and self is an all-pervasive intelligence and existence—what is to be known in meditation. Patañjali has explained that our ignorance leads to a primary misunderstanding that this seer is embedded within the individual medium of *chitta*. Our ignorance develops into a misidentification of the seer as an individual self. This individuality is compounded by many impressions of experience which form our intellect—the way we think and discriminate.

Patañjali described the intellect as the instrument of seeing because we see the world filtered through the beliefs or biases we hold. As the intellect becomes enlivened and appears as if sentient, these modifications sprout, and the individual self becomes further identified with an external sense of self. This stage is described as the seer becoming cognitively blended with the instrument of seeing, which forms *asmita*, the egoistic self.

What we seek to discover through meditation is how we have shifted our experience of self from an all-pervasive intelligence and existence, to an individual form of self, and finally to an egoistic self. For the all-pervasive seer to be established in itself we must unwind the modifications of wrong knowledge. Inverse propagation is unwinding our belief in an egoistic self—"I-am this and that." Once that is unwound, our identity can shift to a pure sense of existence held in the individual medium. This is our *jivatman*, the individual soul or *purusha*, the indweller. Finally, with keen discrimination we experience a state of absorption with "what is to be known" and our identity of self becomes established in all-pervasive self. This is *samadhi*.

Understanding the misidentification of self with the ego begins with the gross body and the physical world. By examining our attachments there, we discover that our egoistic self is an innocent projection of the impressions or beliefs held in the intellect. These wrong notions are what are binding us, and the ego, mind and senses are driven by the beliefs we hold. As we work to gain correct knowledge, the impulses that propel us

---

[151] *Yoga Sūtras* III-5.
[152] *Yoga Sūtras* III-6.

to look outside ourselves for wholeness become quiet. We gain the knowledge that the ego is the agent of our beliefs, and it can surrender to the guidance of the intellect's new knowledge. With the ego quiet, the intellect can shift to looking deeper inside where it forms a new identity of self. The individual soul dawns within.

Gradually, with very keen discrimination, we realize our individual soul as *jivātman*, a pure "I-am." Established in "I-am" we find our way to an unbound, unlimited self, which dwells within each being as the seer. The knowledge and realization of *ātman* as both transcendent and immanent is reached. "I-am" is the personal, immanent experience of the all-pervasive transcendent self. They are both one.

Samyama is applied to subsequent stages only when one has mastered the preceding one. *Samyama* can never be achieved by jumping over the intermediate stages. Absorption in pure consciousness is only attained at the highest stage.

~~~

III-1
deśa-bandhaś cittasya dhāranā
Focusing the mind at one-point is *dhāranā*.

The practice of meditation involves three internal faculties: the mind, ego, and intellect. *Dhāranā*, *dhyāna*, and *samādhi* are the three deeply internal limbs of *astānga yoga*, and they are defined in *sūtras* III-1 through III-3. Patañjali teaches that this group of three practiced together is *samyama*, the perfect regulation of *chitta*.[153] The goal of these practices is the goal of all Yoga: the realization of our real self. In *dhāranā*, we train the mind to fix on one point. When that focus is unwavering, it is called *dhyāna*; and our identification with our real self is *samādhi*.

Dhāranā involves concentrating the mind on any one point, and the point of focus may be external or internal. In *sūtras* I-32 through 40, Patañjali gives a series of one-pointed practices. *Dhāranā* advances internal concentration; a one-pointed mind alleviates obstacles. All methods suggested for the mind train and direct it toward the intellect.

The seer is abstract and imperceptible and cannot be realized at once. We need to establish regular, ongoing practice. To help develop concentration, we can begin by focusing on concrete objects and gradually

---

[153] *Yoga Sūtras* III-4.

shift toward the subtle and abstract. This method leads to stability in the mind and evenness in the intellect. Abiding practice with complete faith and devotion controls the most wavering and restless mind.

To find the seer, we can analyze our experience from gross to subtle. Our body is a bundle of energy. If we analyze every part of the body, we find tissues. These tissues are bundles of cells, and cells are bundles of atoms. An atom is made up of a proton, neutron, and electrons, and all are projections of energy. Our body is a projection of energy, and the space that permeates existence is filled with divine energy. We receive life energy from all-pervasive space in the form of oxygen, our breath. Life energy is unlimited. If we examine life closely, we understand that we live in an ocean of divine energy. It is all around us and within us. This ocean of energy is the cause of the universe and our physical, subtle and causal bodies. When we contemplate energy in this way, we will find our self as separate from energy. We are the seer and we are observing this ocean of energy.

Our minds need help to turn from outside to inside. *Mantras* provide a focus when we practice meditation. These sounds, which seers have realized and shared with us, are related with the internal vibration of the source of life. Just as a seed carries the potential of a certain type of plant, *mantras* are sounds that resonate with certain qualities. When we internally chant a *mantra*, these seeds of vibration release their potential and the quality of the vibration blossoms within, providing the mind with an uplifting focus.

The subtle sound of our breathing produces the sound *soham*. *So* means "that," and is sounded with the inhalation; *ham* means I-am, and is expressed with the exhalation. This *mantra*, *soham*, which is the sound of our breath, continuously indicates, "I am one with that supreme source."[154] With this *mantra*, we elevate our life energy. Through practice, our *prāna* is controlled, which leads to a peaceful, steady mind. This is the foundation for achieving higher levels of consciousness.

~ ~ ~

III-2
tatra pratyayaika-tānatā dhyānam
Prolonged focus on that point is *dhyāna*.

---

[154] *Isa Upanishad* 16.

When we think again and again about any particular object, automatically our minds become one with that.[155] Meditation, *dhyāna*, is the process of putting our mind on one point and holding it there, trying to become one with the point of focus.

We need a sharp, pure, and stable intellect to realize the source of life. To achieve such an intellect, we advance gradually, one step at a time. It is like climbing a tall ladder one rung at a time. We start wherever we can focus our mind, and gradually reach into infinity. To achieve this we have to include our vital energy and emotions. A great misunderstanding is that emotions cease with the practice of meditation.

Both the intellect and the emotions influence behavior. Knowledge is the property of the conscious intellect, and emotions belong to the activity of the ego. Experiences generate a range of emotional responses, including rage, frustration, grief, and joy. In meditation, the intellect guides emotional energy and refines it into devotion. Devotion is a purified form of emotion. As the discerning intellect quiets the mind and guides it toward the self, it also calms emotions and channels their energy back to the source. As we practice meditation, thoughts and feelings continue to arise. Yoga teaches us to stop identifying our self with worldly thoughts and emotions, which frees us to cultivate devotion in the light of knowledge, and to seek the source of our life.

Each human life begins where supreme light manifests in the *brahma chakra* and enlightens the intellect. Life is a projection of energy inspired by the divine light. This light appears in the heart in the form of emotion or love. Light, life and love are interwoven aspects of our being. Much as we try, our love can never be fulfilled in the external world. As long as we exist, we will experience emotion, but we never fulfill our love through people, places and things.

The senses enjoy external objects, and as we become attached to these objects, we create the impression that the objects are valuable and desirable. This impression stimulates the desire to accumulate, which leads to the cycle of enjoyment and suffering. This cycle is the wheel of life known as the *karma chakra*. It circles through desire, action, the fruit of action, and enjoyment or suffering. Desire prompts action. Action brings results. Success leads to joy, and failure to suffering. Fulfilled desires reinforce desire and often lead to greed, while unfulfilled desires lead to

---

[155] *Atharva Veda* 19.51.1.

desperation and anger. These feelings prompt action and this wheel of life goes around and around.

There is a great difference between need and desire. Our needs are our basic requirements in life and these must be fulfilled. Food, clothing, and shelter are some of our basic human needs. Desire causes us to go after unnecessary things, and to collect and hoard them. To end our senseless accumulation and step off the wheel of *karma chakra*, we turn our attention inward and search for the cause of life.

Together, light, life, love, desire, action, fruit and enjoyment make up the wheel of life. The realization that divine light is the cause of life frees us from the *karma chakra*. Light, life and love are related with the inner journey. Desire, action, results and enjoyment are related with the external world. Light, life and love are the hub, and desire, action, fruit and enjoyment are the spokes. As we sit in meditation, we allow desire, action, results, and enjoyment to disperse. Instead, we focus on our search for the source of life: divine light, infinite, all-pervasive consciousness, which enlightens all *chittas*, all intellects, all of us.

When we turn our emotions toward our cause, emotion is transformed into devotion and we realize oneness in all beings. With this realization, hate, jealousy, anger, greed, desire, and lust vanish; and love for all beings awakens. Love is far different from lust. Lusty people may say, "I love you" to fulfill desire, but once their desire is met, they lose their infatuation. If a feeling involves demands or manipulation, it is not love and it is not devotion. Love is devotion; it never demands, it only gives.

Meditation sharpens the intellect and leads to pure wisdom. Pure wisdom helps us realize divine light, the source of life and love. This is the purpose of *dhyāna*: to realize oneness with divine light. We practice *dhārana* again and again to focus our minds on one point. When our contemplation is unwavering, we experience *dhyana*. In *samādhi*, we become absorbed in the source of our life. Our practices require effort; *samādhi* is the result.

~~~

III-3
tad evārtha-mātra-nirbhāsam svarūpa śūnyam iva samādhih
Chitta reflecting as the object alone, as if empty of its own form, is samādhi (complete identification with the pure consciousness).

Samādhi means evenness of intellect. *Samā* is even and *dhi* is intellect. In *samādhi*, the intellect, *chitta*, is without any distortion or movement. It is still

172

and the seer resides in its own qualities—all-pervasive intelligence and existence.

The ultimate goal of Yoga is to be one with the source of life. *Īśvara* is all-pervasive, omniscient, omnipresent, and omnipotent. Bondage and emancipation are related with the intellect. Pure spirit is the witness and illuminator, and cannot be bound. The presence of spirit creates consciousness in the intellect. Spirit is all-pervading—it resides within and surrounds every medium, permeating everything everywhere. Just as we define space by the boundaries we create, we define our existence by the boundaries of nature, and we impose limits on limitless spirit. The limits and boundaries we experience are the construction of our intellect. We feel and think that all-pervading consciousness, experienced as our individual consciousness, is specific to us. In reality it is part and parcel of the all-pervading seer.

Not only does spirit reside in our intellect, but it pervades our whole being. There is no present or presence in which spirit does not exist. It is omnipresent and omniscient, and we experience these qualities of spirit as our own self, our existence. Sāmkhya tells us that this universe is projected by nature in the light of spirit. Spirit pervades all of nature. Spirit's omnipresence may be described as a reflection, a manifestation, or a projection of consciousness into a medium, but we must understand that consciousness does not enter into the medium of *chitta* and become contained there. It is all-pervasive.

All movement and all limitations are related with nature. Spirit, *purusha*, is the observer, the seer. Spirit's all-pervasiveness can never be bound or limited. Therefore, spirit is never bound nor liberated. Bondage and emancipation are related with the individual intellect. Spirit does not take form, nor does it need to be set free. It is our beliefs which create the sense of being bound or free. The intellect is like a gatekeeper who imprisons or releases a person. Being bound or free are in the hands of the guard, not the person imprisoned. Through the intellect, we find the freedom of the seer.

With knowledge and realization, we remove our suffering and limited sense of self and experience an unbound, unlimited self. This freedom is the purpose of knowledge and the methods of Yoga. When we realize the self as distinct from the intellect, and one with *ātman*, we reach *samādhi*, the goal of Yoga. In *sūtra* III-55, Patañjali states this is emancipation—equal purity of the medium and spirit.

Discrimination between the intellect and the self is challenging because the mind, ego, and intellect appear conscious. Scriptures and wise teachers guide our discrimination. Sāmkhya and Yoga teach us that the mind, ego, and intellect, although appearing conscious, are in fact phenomena of nature. They appear conscious because they adopt the qualities of consciousness. Consciousness appears in the media of nature, just as light appears in light bulbs. The intellect, ego and mind are instruments used by the seer, which enlightens these instruments and observes their activities.

This truth is realized through discrimination and wisdom. The goal of practice is freedom from any feeling of lack and separation. They are no longer possible when we realize *atman* pervading our individual medium as the "I-am."

Glossary

-A-

A-	- a prefix meaning "away from" or not
Abhāva	- lack, absence
Abhiniveśa	- fear of death, of loss, of change; see: *kleśa*
Abhyasa	- practice, the effort applied toward finding the source of self
Acharya	- teacher
Adhi-	- a prefix meaning "due to"
Adrista	- visible
Āgamāh	- testimony
Aham	- I-am, pure ego
Āhāra	- all that we receive from the external world through the senses
Ahimsā	- non-violence; one of the five *yamas*
Āyurveda	- one body of the Vedas pertaining to health
Alingam	- unmanifest, causal nature
Anāhat	- unstruck, an epithet for the sound of Om
Ānanda	- blissfulness; a stage of *samādhi*.
Anantam	- infinity
Andha-tāmisra	- blind aversion; *abhiniveśa*
Anumāna	- inferential truth; known through one's own logic.
Aparigraha	- non-accumulation, non-grasping; one of the five *yamas*
Asamprajñatah	- the highest stage of *samādhi*; complete absorption into *Brahman*, the source of both nature and spirit
Āsana	- physical postures; one of the eight limbs of *Astānga Yoga*; *Lit:* stable, easy seat
Asat	- the changing realm of energy and matter; *Lit:* untruth
Astānga Yoga	- the eight-limbed path of yoga
Asteya	- non-stealing; one of the five *yamas*
Asmitā	- egoism
Atha	- now
Ātmā (n)	- the higher self or universal soul

175

Avidyā	- ignorance, the five knots of ignorance, lack of knowledge, nescience; see: *klesa*
Avisesa	- the subtle level; includes ego and the five *tanmātras*
Avyakta	- invisible, unmanifest; refers to nature

-B-

Bandha	- in *hatha yoga*, a hold in the physical body that contains energy and then releases its flow internally
Bhakti Yoga	- the path of devotion
Bhoga	- enjoyment through the senses, mind, and intellect
Bhūta	- the five primordial elements; earth, water, fire, air and space; beings
Brahma chakra	- the highest *chakra* in the body, at the top of the head; the place of the *chitta*
Brahmacarya	- control of emotion, energy; one of the five *yamas*
Brahman	- the unmanifest; one, absolute source
Brahmvritti	- a state of consciousness in which all modes of mind are directed toward the source
Buddhi	- individual intellect, situated in the *brahma chakra*

-C-

Chakra	- centers of energy in the physical body from the base of the spine to the top of the head; from lower to higher, *mūlādhāra, svādhishtān, manipūra, anāhata, vishuddha, lalana, ājña,* and *brahma*
Chit	- intelligence
Chitta	- the first projection of nature; the medium that adopts and reflects consciousness and functions as intellect; located at the top of the head

-D-

Daiva	- divine beings
Dhāranā	- a one-pointed focus in meditation; concentration; one of the eight limbs of *astānga yoga*
Dharma	- an action that supports the life of all beings
Dharmasāstra	- scriptures that describe *dharma*

176

Glossary

Dhyāna	- meditation; a prolonged focus; one of the eight limbs of *astānga yoga.*
Drastā	- seer, purusha
Drsya	- seen
Duhkha	- pain; see: *sukha*
Dvesa	- aversion; see: *rāga* and *klesa*

-E-

Ekāgra	- one-pointed
Ekātattva	- single truth, one principle

-G-

Grahana	- knowledge; instrument of knowledge or intellect.
Grahītā	- knower or ego
Grāhya	- known; object received in the mind
Guna	- quality; three qualities of nature: *sattva, rajas,* and *tamas*

-H-

Hāna	- method to avoid suffering
Hānopāya	- there is a method for the removal of suffering.
Hatha	- pertains to balancing the systems of the body
Heya	- avoidable
Heya hetu	- cause of suffering

-I-

Indriya	- senses; five cognitive and five active senses
Īsvara	- God; special *purusha* untouched by time or action
Īsvara pranidhānā	- surrender to God

-J-

Jīva	- living being
Jīvātmā	- the individual soul
Jñāna	- knowledge

-K-

Kaivalya	- freedom of the seer in the aloneness of seeing
Kapila	- the Vedic seer of the Sāmkhya system of philosophy

Karma	- action
Karmaśayo	- reservoir of results of action
Kleśa	- misery, the five afflictions: ignorance, egoism, attraction, aversion, and fear of death
Kośa	- sheath of the soul
Kriyā Yoga	- an integrated method that includes austerity, self-study, and self-surrender

-L-

Linga, lingam	- first projection of nature; causal form
Loka	- a level of the universe

-M-

Maha	- great
Mahāmoha	- great infatuation; *rāga*
Mahābhārata	- historical Indian epic; includes the *Bhagavad Gītā*
Mahat	- great principal; abbreviation of *mahatattva*
Mahatattva	- cosmic intellect
Maha yoga	- great yoga; a combined path that includes breath, *mantra,* analysis, and surrender
Manas	- mind
Māya	- divine power; limiting power of nature
Moha	- infatuation
Moksha	- liberation of the soul beyond birth and death
Mudrās	- gestures that seal energy

-N-

Neti	- cleansing practices
Nidrā	- sleep
Nirodha	- stilled
Nirvicāra	- a stage of *samprajnātah samādhi*
Nirvitarkā	- a stage of *samprajnātah samādhi*
Niyamas	- personal observances; purity, contentment, austerity, self-study, self-surrender; one limb of *astānga yoga*

-P-

178

Glossary

Param	- supreme
Paramātmā	- supreme soul
Parigraha	- to grasp; accumulate
Parinama duhk	- suffering due to the end of enjoyment
Prajñā	- stable wisdom, pure insight
Prakriti	- nature; energy; three *gunas* in balance
Prāna	- life energy; breath
Pranavah	- designator of Om; breath defined sound
Prānāyāma	- breathing exercises; extension and/or control of breath
Pramāna	- correct evaluation; proof
Pratibha	- intuitive intellect; intellect turned toward its source
Pratyāhāra	- withdrawal of the mind from the senses; one of the eight limbs of *astānga yoga*
Pratyāksha	- perception or cognition; to see or realize truth directly
Purusha	- spirit; indweller; consciousness

-R-

Rāga	- attraction; see: *dvesa* and *klesa*
Rajas, rajoguna	- the quality of action, passion, movement
Rishi	- seer
Ritambharā Prajñā	- a state of intelligence that is truth bearing

-S-

Sadhāka	- practitioner
Sadhāna	- practice
Samādhi	- evenness of intellect; absorption
Samāsa	- brief form
Sāmkhya	- one of the six systems of Indian philosophy that distinguishes nature from spirit and describes the nature of suffering; its companion is Yoga
Samprajñātah	- *samādhi* with I-amness
Samskāra	- impression, memory
Sankalpa	- planning, the formative imagination of thought
Santosa	- contentment; one of the *niyamas*
Sanyoga	- to join different qualities together

179

Sāstras	- scripture
Sat	- truth
Satkāra	- with respect
Satkarma	- action toward fulfilling our inner demand for freedom
Satsānga	- good and pure company
Sattva, sattoguna	- the quality of purity, light
Satya	- truthfulness; one of the five *yamas*
Sauca	- purity; one of the *niyamas*
Savicārā	- *samādhi* with subtle impressions
Sraddhā	- firm faith based on experience
Siddha	- perfected one
Siddhi	- subtle power
Smriti	- memory
Sthiti	- stable
Sukha	- pleasure; see: *duhkha*
Sūtra	- aphorism; *Lit*: thread
Svādhyāya	- self-study; see: *kriyā yoga, niyama*

-T-

Tama	- darkness; *avidyā*
Tamas, tamoguna	- the quality of darkness, inertia, stability
Tāmisra	- hate; *dvesa*
Tanmātra	- subtle matter
Tapa	- jealousy *r*
Tapah	- penance, austerity; see: *kriyā yoga, niyama*

-U-

Upanishad	- teachings from the Vedas that are dialogues between teacher and disciple; *Lit*: to sit near

-V-

Vairāgya	- detachment; paired with practice, *abhyāsa*
Vedas	- *ancient body of knowledge*
Vedānta	- one of the six systems of Indian philosophy
Vidyā	- real knowledge; vs.: *avidyā*, ignorance

Vihāra	- that which we give out; vs.: *āhāra*, what we receive
Vikalpa	- fancy
Vikāra	- transformation, modification
Viksepa	- disruptions in consciousness
Virāt purusha	- cosmic consciousness
Vīrya	- vitality
Viśesa	- gross level of existence including the five elements, the five cognitive senses, the five active senses, and the mind
Vismriti	- forgetfulness
Vitarka	- *samādhi* with gross impressions
Viveka	- discriminative power of wisdom
Viveka-khyāti	- light of discriminative knowledge
Viyoga	- disunion, to come apart; see: *sanyoga, yoga*
Vritti	- fluctuation; thought; modes of the *chitta*; *Lit*: wave
Vyāsa	- description in broad terms

-Y-

Yama	- vows; self-restraint; one of the eight limbs of *astānga yoga*
Yoga	- oneness or union of similar qualities; one of the six systems of Indian philosophy that describes the methods of gaining inner freedom; companion philosophy is Sāmkhya

Bibliography

Audio Lectures of Brahmrishi Vishvatma Bawra

1. Kullu Ashram, Kullu, India; Lectures on *Astānga Yoga*, 1999.
2. Virat Nagar Ashram, Pinjore, India; Lectures on *Kapila's Sāmkhya Sūtras*, 1991.
3. Virat Nagar Ashram, Pinjore, India; Lectures and Notes on *Yoga Sūtras, pada* 1, 2001.
4. Virat Nagar Ashram, Pinjore, India; Lectures on parts of *Yoga Sūtras, pada* 1.
5. Waterloo Ashram, Ontario, Canada; Lectures on *Kapila's Sāmkhya Sūtras*, 1986.
6. Waterloo Ashram, Ontario, Canada; Lectures on *Kriyā Yoga*.

Books based on lectures by Brahmrishi Vishvatma Bawra;

Divine Radiance Press, Chandigarh, India

1. *Basic Principles of Yoga*, Translated and edited by Raj Dubey, 1994.
2. *How to be a Yogi*, Compiled and translated by Krishan Kanta, 1983.
3. *Kapila's Tattva Samāsa*, Compiled and edited by Margot and William Milcetich, 2006.
4. *Science of Absolute Knowledge*, Compiled and translated by Shyam Sehgal, 1996.
5. *Science of Stable Wisdom*, Compiled and edited by Margot Milcetich, 1998.
6. *Yoga for Life*, Compiled and translated by Krishan Kanta; Hindi, 1965; English, 1980.
7. *The Eternal Soul: Commentary on the Katha Upanishad*, Compiled and edited by William Milcetich, 2009.
8. *Yoga in Action*, Compiled and edited by William & Margot Milcetich, 2010.
9. *Samkhya Karika: with Guadapadacarya Bhasya*, Compiled and edited by William Milcetich, 2012.

182

Other Books and Articles

1. *The Principal Upanisads*, S. Radhakrishnan, George Allen & Unwin Ltd., 1953.
2. *Classical Sāmkhya*, Anima Sen Gupta; Munshiram Manoharlal Publishers, 1981.
3. *Essays on Sāmkhya and Other Systems of Indian Philosophy*, Anima Sen Gupta; Munshiram Manoharlal Publishers, 1977.
4. *Six Systems of Hindu Philosophy*, Raghavan Iyer; www.atmajyoti.org
5. *The Bhagavad Gītā*, Transl. by Winthrop Sargeant; State University of New York Press, 1994.
6. *The Sāmkhya Philosophy*, Nandalal Sinha; Oriental Books, 1915; Munshiram Manoharlal Publishers, 1979.
7. *The Science of Yoga*, I. K. Taimni; Theosophical Publishing House, 1961; Quest Books, 1975.
8. *The Yoga Sūtra Workbook*, Vyaas Houston; American Sanskrit Institute, 1995.
9. *Yoga Philosophy of Patañjali*, Swami Hariharananda Aranya; Calcutta University Press 1963; State University of New York Press, 1985.
10. Bill Bryson, *A Short History of Nearly Everything*, Broadway Books a division of Random House, 2003.

Made in the USA
Columbia, SC
22 March 2018